a physical science unit for high-ability learners in grades 3–4

Invitation to Invent

a physical science unit for high-ability learners in grades 3–4

Invitation to Invent

Project Clarion Primary Science Units
Funded by the Jacob K. Javits Program, United States Department of Education

The College of William and Mary
School of Education
Center for Gifted Education
P.O. Box 8795
Williamsburg, VA 23187-8795

Co-Principal Investigators: Bruce A. Bracken & Joyce VanTassel-Baska
Project Directors: Lori Bland, Tamra Stambaugh, & Valerie Gregory
Unit Developers: Elizabeth de Brux & Tamra Stambaugh
Unit Revisions and Editing: Joyce VanTassel-Baska, Steve Coxon, & Lori Bland

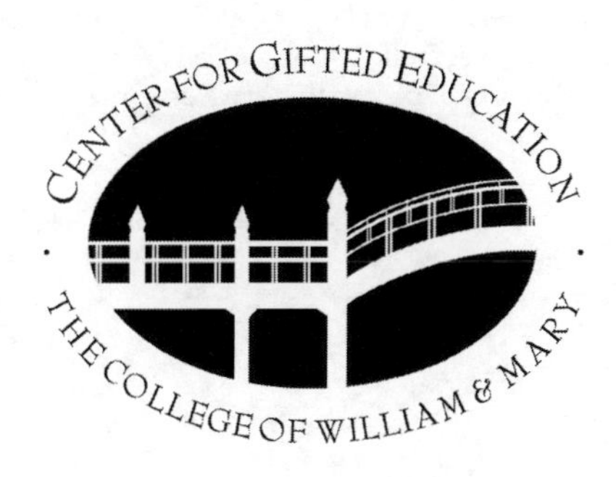

Edited by Lacy Compton
Production Design by Marjorie Parker

ISBN-13: 978-1-59363-391-2
ISBN-10: 1-59363-391-2

Prufrock Press Inc.
P.O. Box 8813
Waco, TX 76714-8813
Phone: (800) 998-2208
Fax: (800) 240-0333
http://www.prufrock.com

Contents

Part I: Unit Overview

Introduction to the Clarion Units

The Project Clarion Science Units for Primary Grades introduce young students to science concepts, science reasoning, and scientific investigation processes. Macroconcepts, such as systems or change, help students connect understanding of science content and processes. The units use a hands-on, constructivist approach that allows children to build their knowledge base and their skills as they explore science topics through play and planned investigations. Students are engaged in creative and critical thinking, problem finding and solving, process skill development, and communication opportunities. Conceptual understanding is reinforced as units strengthen basic language and mathematical concepts, including quantity, direction, position, comparison, colors, letter identification, numbers, counting, size, social awareness, texture, material, shape, time, and sequence.

Introduction to the *Invitation to Invent* Unit

Invitation to Invent, a third- and fourth-grade physical science unit, engages students in a study of the macroconcept of systems to support student learning about simple machines and their uses. Students explore force, motion, and friction as they learn about the six simple machines and how they are put together to form compound machines. The first lesson in the unit introduces students to the role of a scientist. Focusing on the macroconcept of systems, *Invitation to Invent* deepens students' understanding of the scientific concepts in the unit and allows them to try their own hand at using machines for creative problem solving.

Curriculum Framework

The curriculum framework (see Table 1) developed for the Project Clarion science units is based on the Integrated Curriculum Model (ICM), which posits the relatively equal importance of teaching to high-level content, higher order processes and resultant products, and important concepts and issues. The model represents a research-based set of differentiated curricular and instructional approaches found appropriate for high-ability learners (VanTassel-Baska, 1986; VanTassel-Baska & Little, 2003). The framework serves several important functions:

1. The curriculum framework provides scaffolding for the central concept of change, the scientific research process, and the content of the units.
2. The curriculum framework also provides representative statements of advanced, complex, and sophisticated learner outcomes. It demonstrates how a single set of outcomes for all can be translated appropriately for high-ability learners yet can remain accessible to other learners.
3. The curriculum framework provides a way for readers to get a snapshot view of the key emphases of the curriculum in direct relation to each other. The model also provides a way to traverse the elements individually through the continuum of grade levels.

Moreover, the framework may be used to implement the William and Mary units and to aid in new curriculum development based on science reform recommendations.

Table 1
Project Clarion Curriculum Framework for Science Units

Goal	Student Outcomes The student will be able to:
1. Develop concepts related to understanding the world of science.	• Provide examples and salient features of various concepts. • Classify various concepts. • Identify counterexamples of various concepts. • Create definitions or generalizations about various concepts.
2. Develop an understanding of the macroconcept of systems as applied to science content goals.	• Identify the elements of a system. • Determine the boundaries of a system. • Label the inputs and the outputs of a system. • Analyze system interactions.
3. Develop knowledge of selected content topics related to force and motion and simple machines.	• Understand that simple machines are tools that make work easier. • Identify and differentiate the six types of simple machines: screw, wedge, inclined plane, wheel and axle, lever, and pulley. • Identify and classify the simple machines that compose a compound machine. • Explain that motion is an object's direction and speed. • Identify the forces that cause an object's motion. • Explain that friction is a force that opposes motion. • Explain that moving objects have kinetic energy. • Explain that objects capable of kinetic energy due to their position have potential energy.
4. Develop interrelated science process skills.	• Make observations. • Ask questions. • Learn more. • Design and conduct the experiment. • Create meaning. • Tell others what was found.
5. Develop critical thinking skills.	• Describe problematic situations or issues. • Define relevant concepts. • Identify different points of view in situations or issues. • Describe evidence or data supporting a scientific question. • Draw conclusions based on data (making inferences). • Predict consequences.
6. Develop creative thinking skills.	• Develop fluency when naming objects and ideas, based on a stimulus. • Develop flexible thinking. • Elaborate on ideas presented in oral or written form. • Create novel products.
7. Develop curiosity and interest in the world of science.	• Express reactions about discrepant events. • Ask meaningful questions about science topics. • Articulate ideas of interest about science. • Demonstrate persistence in completing science tasks.

Standards Alignment

Each lesson was aligned to the appropriate National Science Education Standards (NSES), Content Standards: K–4 (Center for Science, Mathematics, and Engineering Education [CSMEE], 1996). Table 2 presents detailed information on the alignment between the NSES Content Standards and fundamental concepts within the unit lessons.

Table 2
Invitation to Invent Alignment to National Science Education Standards

Standard	Fundamental Concepts	Unit Lesson
Content Standard A: Abilities necessary to do scientific inquiry	• Ask a question about objects, organisms, and events in the environment. • Plan and conduct a simple investigation. • Employ simple equipment and tools to gather data and extend the senses. • Use data to construct a reasonable explanation. • Communicate investigations and explanations.	1, 2, 3, 4, 5, 6, 7, 8, 9, 10, 11, 12, 13, 14, 15, 16
Content Standard A: Understanding about scientific inquiry	• Scientific investigations involve asking and answering a question and comparing the answer with what scientists already know about the world. • Scientists use different kinds of investigations depending on the questions they are trying to answer. Types of investigations include: describing objects, events, and organisms; classifying them; and doing a fair test (experimenting). • Simple instruments, such as magnifiers, thermometers, and rulers provide more information then scientists obtain using only their senses. • Scientists develop explanations using observations (evidence) and what they already know about the world (scientific knowledge). Good explanations are based on evidence from investigations. • Scientists make the results of their investigations public; they describe the investigation in ways that enable others to repeat the investigation. • Scientists review and ask questions about the results of other scientists' work.	1, 2, 3, 4, 5, 6, 7, 8, 9, 10, 11, 12, 13, 14, 15, 16
Content Standard B: Position and motion of objects	• The position of an object can be described by locating it relative to another object or the background. • An object's motion can be described by tracing and measuring its position over time. • The position and motion of objects can be changed by pushing or pulling. The size of the change is related to the strength of the push or pull.	3, 4, 8, 9, 10, 11, 12, 15, 16
Content Standard E: Abilities of technological design	• Identify a simple problem. • Propose a solution. • Implement proposed solution. • Evaluate a product or design. • Communicate a problem, design, and solution.	5, 6, 7, 13, 14, 15, 16

Macroconcept

The macroconcept for this unit is *systems*. A concept paper on systems is included in Appendix A. The second lesson in this unit introduces the concept of systems. Students are asked to brainstorm examples of systems, categorize their examples, identify "nonexamples" of the concept, and make generalizations about the concept (Taba, 1962). The generalizations about systems incorporated into this unit of study include:

- Systems have parts (elements).
- Systems have boundaries.

- Systems have inputs and outputs.
- The interactions and outputs of a system change when its inputs, elements, or boundaries change.

The concept of systems is integrated throughout the unit lessons and deepens students' understanding of simple machines as systems. Students examine the relationship of important ideas, abstractions, and issues through application of the concept generalizations. For example, the Concluding Questions section of the lesson plans often includes a question that specifically addresses select systems generalizations and requires students to make applications to key science concepts. This higher level thinking enhances the students' ability to "think like a scientist." More information about concept development is provided in Appendix B: Teaching Models.

Key Science Concepts

By the end of this unit, students will understand that:

- Simple machines are tools that make work easier.
- There are six different simple machines: screw, wedge, inclined plane, wheel and axle, lever, and pulley.
- Compound machines combine two or more simple machines.
- Motion is an object's direction and speed.
- Changes in speed or direction of motion are caused by forces.
- Friction is a force that opposes motion.
- Moving objects have kinetic energy.
- Objects capable of kinetic energy due to their position have potential energy.

Practice in using concept maps supports students' learning as they begin to build upon known concepts (Novak & Gowin, 1984). Students begin to add new concepts to their initial understandings of a topic and to make new connections between concepts. The use of concept maps within the lessons also helps teachers to recognize students' conceptual frameworks so that instruction can be adapted as necessary. More information on strategies for using concept mapping, as well as a list of concept mapping practice activities, is provided in Appendix B.

Each Project Clarion unit contains a science concept map (see Figure 1) that displays the key science concepts and the connections students should be able to make as a result of their experiences within the unit. This overview may be useful as a classroom poster that teachers and students can refer to throughout the unit.

Scientific Investigation and Reasoning

The Wheel of Scientific Investigation and Reasoning contains the specific processes involved in scientific inquiry that guide students' thinking and actions. To read more about these processes and suggestions for implementing the wheel into this unit's lessons, see Appendix B.

The lessons that utilize the Wheel of Scientific Investigation and Reasoning include:

- Lesson 1, which helps students gain a better understanding of what scientists do and introduces the Wheel of Scientific Investigation and Reasoning, including the six components of scientific investigation.
- Lessons 3 and 4, which continue the introduction to scientific investigation by requiring students to make observations, ask questions, learn more about

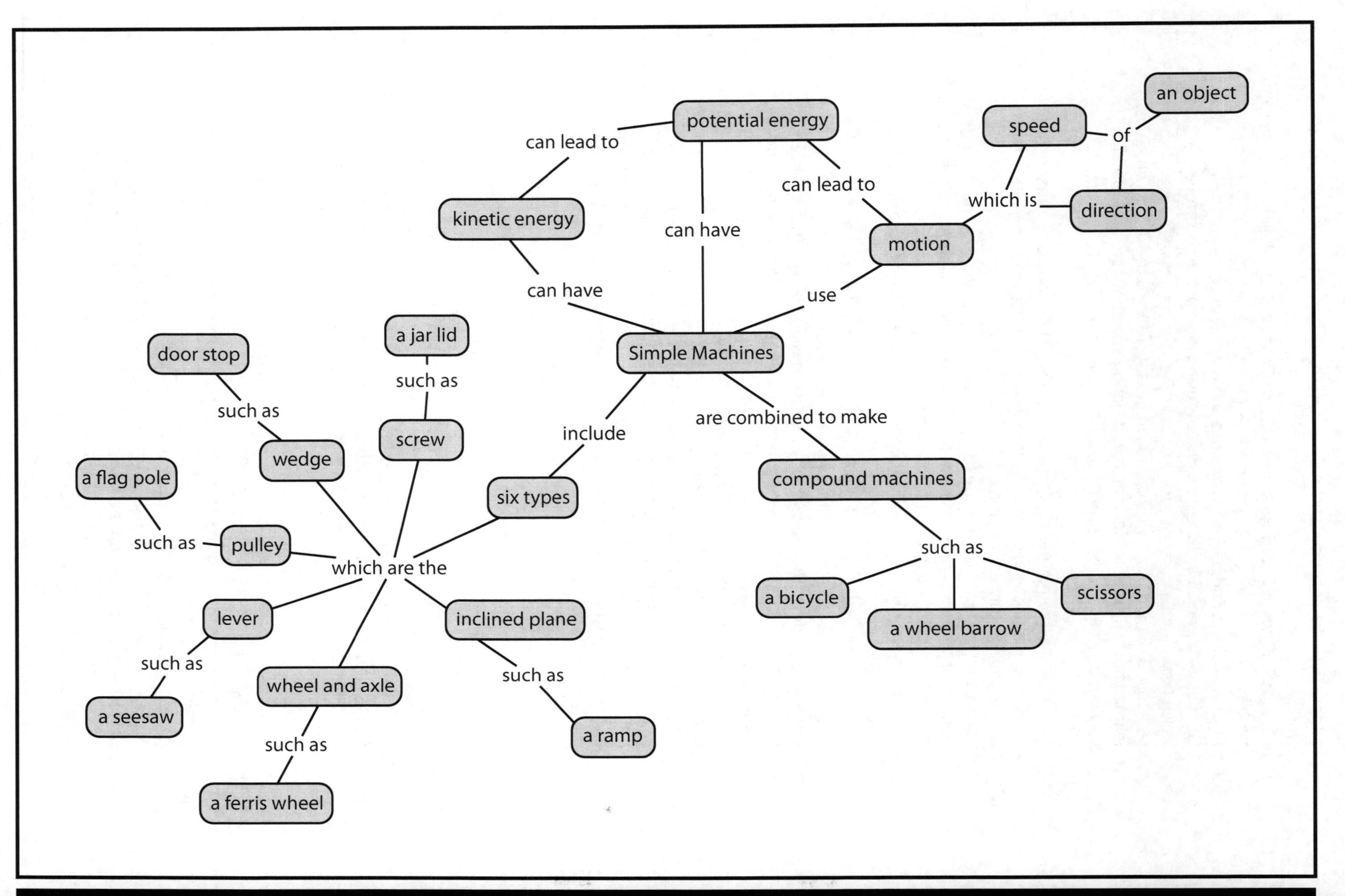

Figure 1. Unit concept map.

a topic, design and conduct an experiment, create meaning, and share their results.
- Lessons 5–7, which introduce students to scaffolding that will enable a creative problem solving process and introduce students to how scientists use creative problem solving and scientific investigation to solve everyday problems.
- Lessons 8–12, which include experiments using each of the six simple machines.
- Lessons 13–16, which provide opportunities for students to employ what they learned from the simple machine investigation and about creative problem solving to invent a compound machine to solve an everyday problem.

Students apply the components of scientific investigation throughout the unit and use the wheel to analyze aspects of an investigation or to plan an investigation. Scientific investigation concepts within the lessons include:
- *Make Observations*: Scientists use their senses as well as instruments to note details, identify similarities and differences, and record changes in phenomena.
- *Ask Questions*: Scientists use information from their observations about familiar objects or events to develop important questions that spark further investigation.
- *Learn More*: Scientists carefully review what is known about a topic and determine what additional information must be sought.
- *Design and Conduct the Experiment*: Scientists design an experiment, which is a fair test of a hypothesis or prediction and is intended to answer a question for a scientific investigation.
- *Create Meaning*: Scientists carefully gather and record data from an experiment, then analyze the data.
- *Tell Others What Was Found*: Scientists communicate findings from an experiment, including a clear description of the question, the hypothesis or prediction, the experiment that was conducted, the data that were collected and how they were analyzed, and the conclusions and inferences that were made from the experiment.

Assessment

The unit includes performance-based assessments for students to complete at the beginning (preassessment) and end (postassessment) of the unit. There are three pre- and postassessments, which assess conceptual understanding, science content knowledge, and application of the scientific investigation process. The preassessment provides baseline data that teachers can use to adjust instructional plans for individual students or groups of students. Preteaching activities accompany selected preassessments.

The postassessment is administered at the completion of the unit and provides valuable information about students' mastery of the targeted objectives and the National Science Education Standards. A rubric is used to score each pre- and postassessment. The pre- and postassessments and dimensions of learning scored for each task include:
- *A macroconcept template, which requires students to draw or write about the macroconcept.* Conceptual understanding is scored on the pre- and postassessments based on the number of appropriate examples of the macroconcept, the elements of the macroconcept, types of the macroconcept listed, and generalizations about the macroconcept.

- *Concept maps, which assess students' content knowledge*. Students are given a prompt for creating a concept map about the unit topic. Understanding of key science concepts is scored on the pre- and postassessments based on the number of appropriate hierarchical levels, propositions, and examples listed.
- *An experimental design template, which requires students to plan an experiment with a given scientific research question*. Students are asked to design an experiment to investigate a question. Students are scored on the pre- and postassessments on their ability to write a prediction or hypothesis, list materials needed for the experiment, list the steps of the experiment in order, and develop a plan to organize data for collection and interpretation.

Teachers also should note that Assessment "Look Fors" are designated in the first section of each lesson plan. The "Look Fors" provide a means for teachers to assess student learning in each lesson. The "Look Fors" are linked to the macroconcept generalizations, key science concepts, and scientific processes identified in each lesson. Teachers can develop checklists for the "Look Fors" or may make informal observations.

Teacher's Guide to Content

The following definitions of key science concepts taught in the unit are described below. A list of content resources and unit glossary also are included.

The Six Simple Machines

People have used simple machines for thousands of years to help them perform work more efficiently. The six simple machines are the screw, the wedge, the inclined plane, the wheel and axle, the lever, and the pulley.

A screw converts circular motion into straight motion. Think of a common flat-head screw. When you rotate the screw using a screwdriver, it moves forward or backward depending on the direction of your motion.

A wedge is a narrow blade that concentrates force and splits whatever it is applied against. Examples include knife blades and log-splitting equipment like wedges and axes.

An inclined plane is essentially a ramp; it reduces the force necessary to raise something from a low level to a higher level or from a high level to a lower level.

A wheel and axle involves a wheel or spoke attached to an axle such that when one is turned, the other must turn as well. Long motions at the edge of the wheel become shorter and more powerful at the axle. Similarly, if the axle is turned, the wheel will move a greater distance. Old-fashioned spinning wheels were essentially wheel and axles.

A lever is a rod that rotates around a pivot. When downward force is applied to the lever on one side, it causes upward motion on the other side. The lever increases the force applied or the distance over which force is applied. Think of a seesaw; if an adult and a child are sitting on either end of the seesaw, the child will not be able to move the adult up easily, but if the adult moves toward the center of the seesaw while the child stays in place, the child will be able to increase the force he or she can apply and raise the adult into the air.

Like a lever, a pulley allows heavy loads to be lifted with less force than would normally be required. One example of a pulley system is a bucket on a rope used to get water out of a well.

Compound Machines

Of course, machines can be much more complex than a screw or wedge. Many machines use combinations of simple machines to perform their job. A machine using a combination of simple machines is called a compound machine. Examples of compound machines are common. Think of a bicycle, which uses wheels and axles, a pulley (chain), a lever (handlebars), and screw fasteners. Other compound machines we use daily include scissors (screw, lever, wedge) and corkscrews (wheel and axle, screw, lever).

Force, Friction, and Motion

Machines amplify the force a person is able to apply to a task. Force is a push or pull that can potentially cause acceleration or change in the motion of an object. Force becomes work when the potential change in motion becomes actual change. If you push a wall, you are applying force to that wall. The wall will not move, however, so you are doing no work. If, on the other hand, you push a chair, the chair will move. In this case, the force is causing the chair to accelerate, so work is being done. Using a machine can increase the force you are able to generate. If you push the chair down an inclined plane or push a chair that has caster wheels, it will accelerate even more with the same amount of effort on your part. At the top of the plane the chair is said to have potential energy. Its position gives it the potential for movement. When it is moving down the plane, it has kinetic energy. The amount of work done can be calculated using a simple equation:

w (work) = F (the force exerted) x d (the distance over which the force is applied)

Friction opposes motion; it causes a moving object to slow down. Friction causes some kinetic energy to become heat. Friction occurs when two objects rub together. When you throw a ball, it "rubs" against the air. The ball's contact with the air causes friction, which slows its motion. Designers often try to minimize friction to improve the speed. Aerodynamic vehicles like race cars are shaped to minimize friction by reducing the rubbing of the air to improve the speed of the vehicle. Grease or similar lubricants are used to reduce friction in gears and bearings. Although friction often is considered undesirable, it is sometimes necessary as well. The brakes on our cars, for instance, depend on friction.

Unit Glossary

Axle: a rod in the center of a wheel, around which the wheel turns.

Compound machine: a combination of two or more simple machines.

Direction: the way that someone or something is moving or pointing.

Force: any action that changes the shape or the movement of an object.

Friction: the force that slows down objects when they rub against each other.

Inclined plane: a flat surface that is raised so one end is higher than the other.

Kinetic energy: the energy of motion.

Lever: a stiff bar that rests on a support called a fulcrum that lifts or moves loads.

Motion: an object's direction and speed.

Potential energy: the energy of objects capable of kinetic energy due to their position.

Pulley: grooved wheels and a rope used to raise, lower, or move a load.

Screw: an inclined plane wrapped around a pole that holds things together or lifts materials.

Simple machines: the six most basic tools that make work easier.

Speed: the rate at which something moves.

Wedge: an inclined plane used to separate objects, lift objects, or hold objects in place.

Wheel: a round frame or object that turns on an axle.

Teaching Resources

Required Resources (used in relevant lessons)

Brown, S. G. (2004). *Professor Aesop's the crow and the pitcher*. Berkeley, CA: Tricycle Press.
Jones, C. F. (1994). *Mistakes that worked*. New York: Doubleday.
Lehn, B. (1998). *What is a scientist?* Brookfield, CT: The Millbrook Press.
Scholastic. (1996). *Scholastic children's dictionary* (Rev. ed.). New York: Author.

Additional Resources

Bridgman, R., & MacLeod, J. (2006). *How nearly everything was invented*. New York: DK Children.
Hodge, D. (1998). *Simple machines*. New York: Kids Can Press.
Macaulay, D. (1998). *The new way things work*. New York: Houghton Mifflin.
St. George, J. (2005). *So you want to be an inventor*? New York: Puffin.
Tocci, S. (2003). *Experiments with motion*. New York: Scholastic.
Woods, M., & Woods, M. B. (1999). *Ancient machines: From wedges to waterwheels*. Minneapolis, MN: Runestone Press.

Useful Websites

Downey, L. (2008). *Levi Strauss: A short biography*. Retrieved from http://www.levistrauss.com/Downloads/History_Levi_Strauss_Biography.pdf
The Museum of Science. (1997). *The elements of machines*. Retrieved from http://www.mos.org/sln/Leonardo/InventorsToolbox.html
Nave, R. (n.d.). *Force*. Retrieved from http://hyperphysics.phy-astr.gsu.edu/hbase/force.html#defor
Pulley basics. (n.d.). Retrieved from http://www.the-office.com/summerlift/pulleybasics.htm
Rube Goldberg. (n.d.). Retrieved from http://www.rube-goldberg.com
Simple machines. (n.d.). Retrieved from http://www.nvsd44.bc.ca/sites/ReportsViewOnePopM.asp?RID=3812

Part II: Lesson Plans

Lesson Plans

Overview of Lessons

An overview of the lessons is provided in Table 3. The overview shows the primary emphasis of each lesson in the unit according to the macroconcept, key science concepts, or the scientific investigation process. Lessons also may have a secondary emphasis, which is listed in the planning section of each lesson, labeled "Planning the Lesson."

Table 3
Overview of Lessons

Concept of Systems	Scientific Process	Key Science Concepts
	Preassessment	
	Lesson 1: What Is a Scientist?	
Lesson 2: What Is a System?		
	Lesson 3: What Scientists Do—Observe, Question, Learn More	
	Lesson 4: What Scientists Do—Experiment, Create Meaning, Tell Others	
	Lesson 5: Creative Problem Solving	
	Lesson 6: The Process of Invention	
	Lesson 7: The Mother of Invention	
		Lesson 8: Introduction to Simple Machines
		Lesson 9: The Screw and the Wedge
		Lesson 10: The Inclined Plane and the Wheel and Axle
		Lesson 11: The Lever
		Lesson 12: The Pulley
		Lesson 13: Compound Machines
	Lesson 14: Final Touches	
	Lesson 15: Invention Fair	
	Lesson 16: Wrap It Up!	
	Postassessment	

Lesson Plan Blueprint

The lesson plan blueprint (see Table 4) for each lesson shows:

- instructional purpose,
- generalizations about the macroconcept of systems,
- key science concepts,
- scientific investigation skills and processes, and
- assessment "Look Fors."

Table 4
Lesson Plan Blueprint

Lesson #	Title	Instructional Purpose	Systems Generalizations	Key Science Concepts	Scientific Investigation Skills and Processes	Assessment "Look Fors" Students should be able to:
	Preassessment					
1	*What Is a Scientist?*	• To learn the characteristics of scientists and the investigation skills that scientists use.			• Make observations. • Ask questions. • Learn more. • Design and conduct the experiment. • Create meaning. • Tell others what was found.	• Identify the scientific investigation processes used by scientists.
2	*What Is a System?*	• To understand the concept of systems. • To understand four generalizations of systems.	• Systems have parts (elements). • Systems have boundaries. • Systems have inputs and outputs. • The interactions and outputs of a system change when its inputs, elements, or boundaries change.	• Simple machines are tools that make work easier. • Compound machines combine two or more simple machines.		• Provide examples of systems. • Categorize examples of systems, explaining their reasoning. • Show understanding of the concept of "generalization." • Provide an example for a system generalization. • Provide nonexamples of systems.
3	*What Scientists Do—Observe, Question, Learn More*	• To apply three of six scientific investigation processes (Make Observations, Ask Questions, Learn More) described in the Wheel of Scientific Investigation and Reasoning. • To understand force, motion, and friction.	• Systems have parts (elements). • Systems have boundaries. • Systems have inputs and outputs. • The interactions and outputs of a system change when its inputs, elements, or boundaries change.	• Motion is an object's direction and speed. • Changes in speed or direction are caused by forces. • Moving objects have kinetic energy. • Objects capable of kinetic energy due to their position have potential energy.	• Make observations. • Ask questions. • Learn more.	• Apply the steps of the scientific process. • Define motion, force, kinetic and potential energy, and friction and state examples.
4	*What Scientists Do—Experiment, Create Meaning, Tell Others*	• To apply three of six investigation processes (Design and Conduct the Experiment, Create Meaning, Tell Others What Was Found) described in the Wheel of Scientific Investigation and Reasoning to design and conduct an experiment about speed, motion, and friction using toy cars.	• Systems have parts (elements). • Systems have boundaries. • Systems have inputs and outputs. • The interactions and outputs of a system change when its inputs, elements, or boundaries change.	• Motion is an object's direction and speed. • Changes in speed or direction are caused by forces. • Friction is a force that opposes motion. • Moving objects have kinetic energy. • Objects capable of kinetic energy due to their position have potential energy.	• Make observations. • Ask questions. • Learn more. • Design and conduct the experiment. • Create meaning. • Tell others what was found.	• Define motion, force, kinetic and potential energy, and friction and state examples. • Apply the steps of the scientific process. • Interpret data from a data table. • Describe how the experiment was conducted and what results were found.
5	*Creative Problem Solving*	• To facilitate students' learning of the creative problem solving process as a way to scaffold invention strategies.	• Systems have parts (elements). • Systems have boundaries. • Systems have inputs and outputs. • The interactions and outputs of a system change when its inputs, elements, or boundaries change.			• Understand the creative problem solving process. • Use the creative problem solving process.

Table 4, continued

Lesson #	Title	Instructional Purpose	Systems Generalizations	Key Science Concepts	Scientific Investigation Skills and Processes	Assessment "Look Fors" Students should be able to:
6	*The Process of Invention*	• To provide support and scaffolding for students to create a new invention.	• Systems have parts (elements). • Systems have boundaries. • Systems have inputs and outputs. • The interactions and outputs of a system change when its inputs, elements, or boundaries change.			• Engage successfully in fluency, flexibility, and elaboration of their ideas. • Work in small groups to come up with an original change to the car.
7	*The Mother of Invention*	• To invent a product that will solve a problem encountered in everyday life using the scaffolds provided for research and problem-solving skills.	• Systems have parts (elements). • Systems have boundaries. • Systems have inputs and outputs. • The interactions and outputs of a system change when its inputs, elements, or boundaries change.	• Simple machines are tools that make work easier. • Compound machines combine two or more simple machines.	• Ask questions. • Learn more.	• Apply the steps of scientific investigation.
8	*Introduction to Simple Machines*	• To identify that there are six simple machines. • To investigate the purpose and need for simple machines.	• Systems have parts (elements). • Systems have boundaries. • Systems have inputs and outputs.	• Simple machines are tools that make work easier. • There are six different simple machines.	• Make observations. • Create meaning. • Tell others what was found.	• Identify various types of simple machines. • Use terms such as parts, boundaries, inputs, and outputs when discussing simple machines.
9	*The Screw and the Wedge*	• To identify the nature and purpose of the screw and wedge. Emphasis will be placed on identifying the screw and the wedge as two simple machines, including purposes for use. • To investigate why a screw is better than a nail to hold two pieces of wood together.	• Systems have parts (elements). • Systems have boundaries. • Systems have inputs and outputs.	• Simple machines are tools that make work easier. • There are six different simple machines.	• Make observations. • Ask questions. • Learn more. • Design and conduct the experiment. • Create meaning. • Tell others what was found.	• Identify various types of screws as simple machines. • Identify various types of wedges as simple machines. • Use terms such as parts, boundaries, inputs, and outputs when discussing whether a screw or a wedge is a system. • Record data correctly as part of an experiment. • Articulate findings from an experiment to other class members.
10	*The Inclined Plane and the Wheel and Axle*	• To identify two new simple machines and their purposes: the inclined plane and the wheel and axle. • To investigate the best height of an inclined plane for a car to travel the farthest.	• The interactions and outputs of a system change when its inputs, elements, or boundaries change.	• Simple machines are tools that make work easier. • There are six different simple machines. • Motion is an object's direction and speed. • Friction is a force that opposes motion. • Moving objects have kinetic energy. • Objects capable of kinetic energy due to their position have potential energy.	• Make observations. • Ask questions. • Learn more. • Design and conduct the experiment. • Create meaning. • Tell others what was found.	• Accurately measure and record the distance traveled by the car and the height of the inclined plane. • Accurately use words such as friction, speed, distance, inclined plane, and wheel and axle in discussion. • Generate ideas or examples of inclined planes and wheel and axles.

Table 4, continued

Lesson #	Title	Instructional Purpose	Systems Generalizations	Key Science Concepts	Scientific Investigation Skills and Processes	Assessment "Look Fors" Students should be able to:
11	*The Lever*	• To identify a new simple machine and its purposes: the lever. • To conduct a simple experiment to determine the best fulcrum and load placement for the easiest lift.	• The interactions and outputs of a system change when its inputs, elements, or boundaries change.	• Simple machines are tools that make work easier. • There are six different simple machines. • Changes in speed or direction of motion are caused by forces.	• Make observations. • Ask questions. • Learn more. • Design and conduct the experiment. • Create meaning. • Tell others what was found.	• Follow directions to set up a simple experiment. • Measure and record data accurately. • Use appropriate science terms such as speed, kinetic and potential energy, motion, lever, and fulcrum. • Draw appropriate conclusions after conducting investigations. • Identify and explain the parts and interactions of a system.
12	*The Pulley*	• To introduce students to pulleys and how they are used to lift heavy objects. • To conduct a simple investigation to determine that the more pulleys used, the easier an object is to lift.	• The interactions and outputs of a system change when its inputs, elements, or boundaries change.	• Simple machines are tools that make work easier. • There are six different simple machines. • Motion is an object's direction and speed. • Changes in speed or direction of motion are caused by forces. • Friction is a force that opposes motion. • Moving objects have kinetic energy. • Objects capable of kinetic energy due to their position have potential energy.	• Make observations. • Ask questions. • Learn more. • Design and conduct the experiment. • Create meaning. • Tell others what was found.	• Follow directions to make a pulley. • Explain the difference between the types of pulleys and their benefits. • Recognize friction in using pulleys. • Articulate the benefits and drawbacks of using pulleys. • Define motion, force, kinetic and potential energy, and friction and state examples.
13	*Compound Machines*	• To identify how the six machines may be combined to create compound machines. • To solve a given scenario problem using a simple or compound machine as a solution.	• Systems have parts (elements). • Systems have boundaries. • Systems have inputs and outputs.	• Simple machines are tools that make work easier. • There are six different simple machines. • Motion is an object's direction and speed. • Changes in speed or direction of motion are caused by forces. • Friction is a force that opposes motion. • Moving objects have kinetic energy. • Objects capable of kinetic energy due to their position have potential energy.	• Make observations. • Ask questions. • Learn more. • Design and conduct the experiment. • Create meaning. • Tell others what was found. • Define motion, force, kinetic and potential energy, and friction and state examples.	• Quickly identify which simple machines or combinations of simple machines may be needed to make work easier. • Articulate and demonstrate how they would use a simple or compound machine. • Define motion, force, kinetic and potential energy, and friction and state examples.

Table 4, continued

Lesson #	Title	Instructional Purpose	Systems Generalizations	Key Science Concepts	Scientific Investigation Skills and Processes	Assessment "Look Fors" Students should be able to:
14	*Final Touches*	• To finalize their inventions in preparation for their invention presentation.	• Systems have parts (elements). • Systems have boundaries. • Systems have inputs and outputs. • The interactions and outputs of a system change when its inputs, elements, or boundaries change.	• Simple machines are tools that make work easier. • There are six different simple machines. • Compound machines combine two or more simple machines. • Motion is an object's direction and speed. • Changes in speed or direction of motion are caused by forces. • Friction is a force that opposes motion. • Moving objects have kinetic energy. • Objects capable of kinetic energy due to their position have potential energy.	• Create meaning.	• Define motion, force, kinetic and potential energy, and friction and state examples. • Apply the steps of the scientific process. • Explain their invention.
15	*Invention Fair*	• To do the invention presentation. • To begin to review the unit principles, including key science concepts and concept generalizations.	• Systems have parts (elements). • Systems have boundaries. • Systems have inputs and outputs. • The interactions and outputs of a system change when its inputs, elements, or boundaries change.	• Simple machines are tools that make work easier. • There are six different simple machines. • Compound machines combine two or more simple machines. • Motion is an object's direction and speed. • Changes in speed or direction of motion are caused by forces. • Friction is a force that opposes motion. • Moving objects have kinetic energy. • Objects capable of kinetic energy due to their position have potential energy.	• Tell others what was found.	• Define motion, force, kinetic and potential energy, and friction and state examples. • Identify and explain the parts of their invention as it relates to systems. • Classify, sort, and label the six different simple machines. • Explain or demonstrate friction, force, motion, direction, kinetic and potential energy and speed as they relate to simple and compound machines.
16	*Wrap It Up!*	• To continue reviewing the unit principles, including key science concepts and concept generalizations. • To summarize content, scientific process, and conceptual understanding.	• Systems have parts (elements). • Systems have boundaries. • Systems have inputs and outputs. • The interactions and outputs of a system change when its inputs, elements, or boundaries change.	• Simple machines are tools that make work easier. • There are six different simple machines. • Compound machines combine two or more simple machines. • Motion is an object's direction and speed. • Changes in speed or direction of motion are caused by forces. • Friction is a force that opposes motion. • Moving objects have kinetic energy. • Objects capable of kinetic energy due to their position have potential energy.	• Make observations. • Ask questions. • Learn more. • Design and conduct the experiment. • Create meaning. • Tell others what was found.	• Provide examples of systems. • Define motion, force, kinetic and potential energy, and friction and state examples. • Identify and classify various types of simple machines. • Use the scientific investigation processes used by scientists.
	Postassessment					

Preteaching Lesson: Science Safety

Planning the Lesson

Instructional Purpose

- To instill in students the importance of safety in the classroom.
- To outline science safety rules to be implemented throughout the unit.

Instructional Time

- 45 minutes

Materials/Resources/Equipment

- Sample materials:
  - Plant
  - Plastic bag of nonhazardous powdery substance (e.g., sugar)
  - Closed jar of nonhazardous liquid (e.g., water)

- Plastic disposable gloves
- Safety goggles
- Chart paper
- Markers
- Science Safety Guidelines (Handout 0A)
- Science Safety Rules printed on chart paper (Handout 0B)

Implementing the Lesson

1. Display sample materials on a long table in front of students. Inform students that they soon will begin a science unit in which they will observe and study many different kinds of materials, such as these. Explain that it is important for students to practice safety during the investigations. Relate the necessity of science safety rules to those of the classroom and physical education.
2. Display and define each item. Tell students that as a class they will create a list of rules they should follow when handling these materials. Have students think of how they can keep their bodies safe. Record these examples on chart paper.
3. Next, unveil the Science Safety Guidelines (Handout 0A) on chart paper. Have students compare the two lists. How do students' examples relate to these rules? If necessary, add additional rules to the list.
4. Explain why some materials (such as knives) or elements (such as fire) are never appropriate for children to handle in school. Briefly discuss the potential hazards associated with these.
5. Finally, conduct a brief demonstration to illustrate how to practice safety guidelines. Take the plastic bag containing a nonhazardous powdery substance and the jar of nonhazardous liquid. Explain that you are going to investigate how the two materials interact. Ask students how you can be safe while doing this investigation. Reinforce that substances can be harmful to the eyes or skin and that they should **never** be ingested. Explain that the same is

true of plants, which can be toxic to humans. Emphasize that students should follow similar guidelines when studying plants in other science units.

6. Following students' examples of safety measures, demonstrate how to use safety goggles to protect the eyes, plastic gloves to protect the hands, and other relevant protective measures, such as pulling long hair back and wearing appropriate clothing. Conduct the demonstration by carefully pouring the powdery substance into the jar of liquid. Emphasize that you should never touch your face or mouth (and especially should not eat or drink) during science experiments.
7. Tell students that materials will be disposed of properly by the teacher after the investigation is completed. Students should not touch any potentially harmful substances.
8. Demonstrate the final rule, "Wash your hands," by properly removing the gloves (without the outside of the gloves ever touching the body) and the goggles. If there is a sink in the classroom, demonstrate how to properly wash one's hands. If no sink is present, inform students that after each investigation the class will go to the bathroom to wash their hands.
9. Conclude the lesson by emphasizing that science investigations are interesting and fun, but they also can be dangerous if not conducted properly. By following the Science Safety Rules, the class will enjoy the benefits of learning about science.

Handout 0A
Science Safety Guidelines

1. Know and follow your school's policies and procedures regarding classroom safety.
2. Always provide direct adult supervision when students are engaging in scientific experimentation.
3. Ensure that all materials and equipment are safe for handling by primary students.
4. Exert extra caution when materials have the potential for harm when used improperly.
5. Use protective gear for eyes, skin, and breathing when conducting experiments, and require students to do the same.
6. Always conduct an experiment by yourself before completing it with the students.
7. Store materials for experiments out of the reach of students.
8. Never allow students to eat or drink during science experiments.
9. Follow general safety rules for sharp objects, heated items, breakables, or spilled liquids.
10. Teach students that it is unsafe to touch their face, mouth, eyes, or other body parts when they are working with plants, animals, microorganisms, or chemicals. Wash hands prior to touching anything. Caution students about putting anything in their mouth or breathing in the smell of substances.
11. Be aware of students' allergies to plants (including plant pollen), animals, foods, chemicals, or other substances to be used in the science classroom. Take all precautions necessary. Common food allergens include peanuts, tree nuts (cashews, almonds, walnuts, hazelnuts, macadamia nuts, pecans, pistachios, and pine nuts), shellfish, fish, milk, eggs, wheat, and soy.
12. Use caution with plants. Never allow students to pick or handle any unknown plants, leaves, flowers, seeds, or berries. Use gloves to touch unknown plants. Many common house, garden, and wooded area plants are toxic.
13. Avoid glass jars and containers. Use plastic, paper, or cloth containers.
14. Thermometers should be filled with alcohol, not mercury.
15. Clearly label any chemicals used and dispose of properly.
16. Teach students safety rules for science (see Handout 0B), including:
    a. **Always** do scientific experiments with an adult present.
    b. **Never** mix things together (liquids, powders) without adult approval.
    c. **Use** your senses carefully. Protect your eyes, ears, nose, mouth, and skin.
    d. **Wash your hands** after using materials for an experiment.

Handout 0B

Science Safety Rules

1. **Always** do scientific experiments with an adult present.

2. **Never** mix things together (liquids, powders) without adult approval.

3. **Use** your senses carefully. Protect your eyes, ears, nose, mouth, and skin.

4. **Wash your hands** after using materials for an experiment.

Preassessment

Planning the Lesson

Instructional Purpose

- To determine prior knowledge of unit content.
- To build understanding of unit macroconcept, science content, and science processes.

Instructional Time

- Macroconcept assessment: 20 minutes
- Science content assessment: 30 minutes, including preteaching activity
- Scientific process assessment: 20 minutes

Materials/Resources/Equipment

- Copies of Preassessment for Systems Concept, Preassessment for Key Science Concepts, and the Preassessment for the Scientific Process, and blank concept map for each student
- Rubric 1 (Scoring Rubric for Systems Concept), Preteaching for Key Science Concepts Preassessment, Sample Concept Map, Rubric 2 (Scoring Rubric for Science Content), and Rubric 3 (Scoring Rubric for Scientific Process) for your use
- Pencils
- Large chart paper
- Drawing paper for each student

Implementing the Lesson

1. Each assessment should be administered on a different day.
2. Explain to students that the class is beginning a new unit of study. Tell them that they will be completing a preassessment to determine what they already know about the topic. Assure them that the assessment is not for a grade and encourage them to do their best.
3. Collect all of the preassessments. Briefly review each assessment and discuss some of the responses in general, indicating that this unit will provide them with more knowledge and skills than they now have.

Scoring

- Score the preassessments using the rubrics provided. Keep the scores and assessments for diagnostic purposes to organize groups for various activities during the unit and to compare pre- and postassessment results.

Name:______________________________ Date:__________

Preassessment for Systems Concept

1. Give five examples of things that are systems.

2. Draw one example of a system that you know.

3. Label at least five features of your system.

4. What are three things you can say about *all* systems?

All systems ____

____

All systems ____

____

All systems ____

____

Name:______________________________ Date:_______________

Rubric 1
Scoring Rubric for Systems Concept

Directions for Use: Score students on their responses to each of the questions.

	5	4	3	2	1
Examples of the Macroconcept	Five or more appropriate examples are given.	Four appropriate examples are given.	Three appropriate examples are given.	Two appropriate examples are given.	One appropriate example is given.
Drawing of the Macroconcept	The drawing contains a recognizable system, with functioning parts.	The drawing contains most of the major elements of the system.	The drawing contains some elements of the system.	The drawing contains a few elements of the system.	The drawing contains only one element.
Features of the Macroconcept	The drawing contains at least five elements or other features of a system.	The drawing contains four elements or other features of a system.	The drawing contains three elements or other features of a system.	The drawing contains two elements or other features of a system.	The drawing contains one element or other feature of a system.
Generalization About the Macroconcept	Three appropriate generalizations are made about systems.	Three somewhat appropriate generalizations are made about systems.	Two appropriate generalizations are made about systems.	One appropriate generalization is made about systems.	Only a statement about systems is made.

Total points possible: 20

Preteaching for Key Science Concepts Preassessment

Directions for the Teacher: Say the following bolded directions to students. Directions for you are not bolded.

Sometimes we know a lot about something even before our teachers teach it in school. Sometimes we don't know very much at all, but we like to learn new things.

For example, what would you think about if someone asked you to tell all you know about how *farms* work? What are some of the words you would use?

(List these on a chart.)

What are some of the things that happen on a farm?

(List these on a chart.)

I am going to show you a way I might tell all I know about how farms work.

(Begin a concept map on a large sheet of paper, using pictures and words, making simple links, and emphasizing these links; see Figure 2 for an example.)

Make your own concept maps on your drawing paper. This practice activity can be done with a partner.

(Share some of the resulting concept maps, encouraging students to articulate their links.)

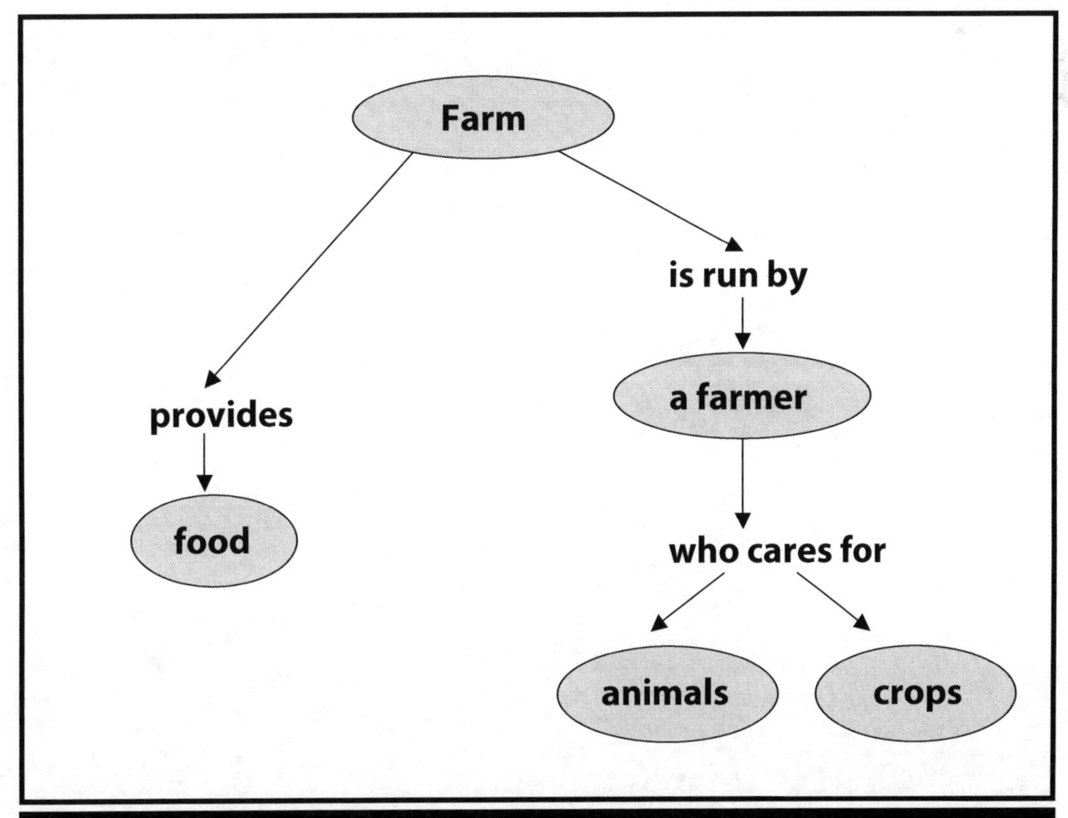

Figure 2. Concept map of farm.

Preassessment for Key Science Concepts

Directions to the Teacher: Read the following paragraph to the students.

> Today I would like you to think about all of the things you know about simple machines. Think about the words you would use and the pictures you could draw to make a concept map. Think about the connections you can make. On your concept map paper, draw in pictures and words all that you know about simple machines. You will be drawing a concept map, just like the ones you did when we discussed the farm. Tell me everything you know about simple machines.

Name:________________________ Date:______________

Concept Map

Simple Machines

Sample Concept Map for Simple Machines

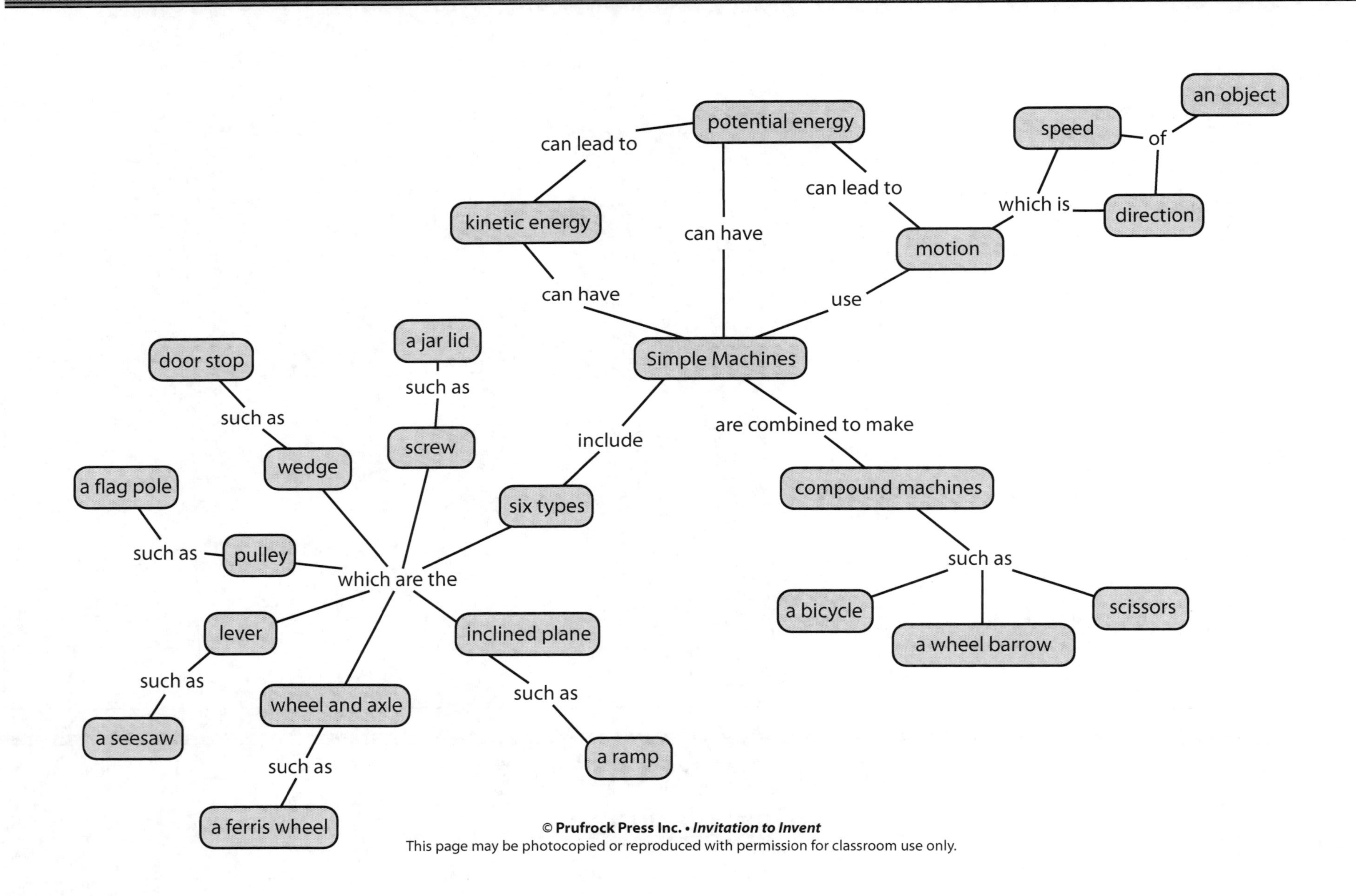

Name:____________________ Date:____________

Rubric 2
Scoring Rubric for Science Content

Directions for Use: Score students on their completed maps.

	5	4	3	2	1	0
Hierarchical Level Each subordinate concept is more specific and less general than the concept drawn above it. Count the number of levels included in the total map.	Five or more levels are identified.	Four levels are identified.	Three levels are identified.	Two levels are identified.	One level is identified.	No hierarchical levels are identified.
Propositions The linking of two concepts indicating a clear relationship is given. Count the total number of propositions identified on the total map.	Twelve or more propositions are provided.	Ten to twelve propositions are provided.	Seven to nine propositions are provided.	Four to six propositions are provided.	One to three propositions are provided.	No propositions are provided.
Examples A valid example of a concept is provided. Count the total number of examples.	Twelve or more examples are provided.	Ten to twelve examples are provided.	Seven to nine examples are provided.	Four to six examples are provided.	One to three examples are provided.	No examples are provided.

Total points possible: 15

Name:______________________________ Date:__________

Preassessment for Scientific Process

Directions: How would you study the question: Are plants attracted to the sun? Describe an experiment to test this question that includes the following:

1. Prediction regarding the question (Are plants attracted to the sun?):

   I predict that ____

   ____

   ____

   ____.

2. What materials will be needed to conduct the experiment?

   ____________________ ____________________

   ____________________ ____________________

   ____________________ ____________________

3. What steps must be taken to conduct the experiment and *in what order*?

   a. ____

   b. ____

   c. ____

   d. ____

   e. ____

4. What data do you want to collect and how should they be recorded?

What will I collect?	How will I record the data?

5. How do the data help me decide if my prediction is correct? Explain.

____

____

____

____

Name:______________________________ Date:_______________

Rubric 3
Scoring Rubric for Scientific Process

Directions for Use: Score students on the responses to each of the questions.

	Criteria	Strong Evidence 3	Some Evidence 2	Little Evidence 1	No Evidence 0
1	**Generates a Prediction**	Clearly generates a prediction appropriate to the experiment.	Somewhat generates a prediction appropriate to the experiment.	Generates an inappropriate prediction.	Fails to generate a prediction.
2	**Lists Materials Needed**	Provides an inclusive and appropriate list of materials.	Provides a partial list of materials needed.	Provides inappropriate materials.	Fails to provide a list of materials needed.
3	**Lists Experiment's Steps**	Clearly and concisely lists four or more steps as appropriate for the experiment design.	Clearly and concisely lists one to three steps as appropriate for the experiment design.	Generates inappropriate steps.	Fails to generate steps.
4	**Arranges Steps in Sequential Order**	Lists steps in sequential order.	Lists most of the steps or one step out of order.	Lists one or two steps or steps are placed in an illogical order.	Does not list steps.
5	**Plans Data Collection**	Clearly states a plan for data collection, including what data will be needed and how they will be recorded.	States a partial plan for data collection, citing some items for collection and some way of recording data.	Provides a minimal plan for either data collection and/or recording.	Fails to identify any part of a plan for data collection.
6	**States Plan for Interpreting Data for Making Predictions**	Clearly states a plan for interpreting data by linking data to prediction.	States a partial plan for interpreting data that links data to prediction.	Provides a brief statement that partially addresses use of data for prediction.	Fails to state a plan for using data for making a prediction.

Total points possible: 18

Note. Adapted from Fowler (1990).

Lesson 1:
What Is a Scientist?

Planning the Lesson

Instructional Purpose

- To learn the characteristics of scientists and the investigation skills that scientists use.

Instructional Time

- 45 minutes

Scientific Investigation Skills and Processes

- Make observations.
- Ask questions.
- Learn more.
- Design and conduct the experiment.
- Create meaning.
- Tell others what was found.

Assessment "Look Fors"

- Students should be able to identify the scientific investigation processes used by scientists.

Materials/Resources/Equipment

- Lab coat for teacher
- One lab coat (white adult T-shirt or dress shirt) for each student
- Beaker
- Microscope or magnifying glass
- PowerPoint slides, charts, or transparencies of Handouts 1A (Completed Frayer Model of Vocabulary Development on Scientists), 1B (Incomplete Frayer Model of Vocabulary Development on Scientists), and 1C (Wheel of Scientific Investigation and Reasoning)
- One chart of Handout 1B for each group of three or four students
- Markers
- Student log books
- *Professor Aesop's the Crow and the Pitcher* by Stephanie Gwyn Brown
- Word wall cards: scientist, communicate, observation, question, experiment

Implementing the Lesson

1. Put on a lab coat. Explain that the students are going to be learning about how scientists study force and motion and how they create compound machines out of simple machines to solve everyday problems.
2. Pick up a beaker and microscope or magnifying glass. Ask the students what kind of job you might have. Explain that you are a scientist. Ask the students if they know a scientist and allow them to discuss what they know about scientists or their experiences with scientists. Record student responses to the following questions:

- Do you know a scientist?
- What do you think scientists do?

3. Display the Completed Frayer Model of Vocabulary Development on Scientists (Handout 1A). Cover entries in each section with sticky notes so students cannot read them until the appropriate time. Ask the students to define a scientist. Write down their definition on the board.
4. Uncover the definition section of the Frayer graphic to reveal the following definition: "a person who studies nature and the physical world by testing, experimenting, and measuring" (Scholastic, 1996) and ask the class to compare and contrast the "official definition" with the class definition.
5. Divide the class into small groups of three or four students. Explain and assign roles to each student in the group: recorder, reporter, supporter (manages materials, keeps the group on task, and encourages), and timekeeper.
6. Give each group the Frayer graphic (Handout 1B) on chart paper with the definition in the appropriate section. Ask groups to write down what a scientist does in the appropriate section (scientific processes). Have reporters share group answers with the class.
7. Uncover the section titled "What Scientists Do" to show the science process skills. Allow students to compare and contrast what they wrote down with the list below. Quickly explain each, adding that they will learn more in the science unit.
   - Make observations.
   - Ask questions.
   - Learn more.
   - Design and conduct the experiment.
   - Create meaning.
   - Tell others what was found.

8. Explain that there are many different types of scientists. Have groups write down types of scientists. Groups should share their responses with the class and then compare and contrast them with the types listed on the large group chart in the "Examples" section. Note that each word ends with the suffix "ist" and that this suffix means "a person who."
9. Repeat the process in #8, asking the students to give nonexamples of scientists and then share their responses. Then uncover the section of the chart titled "Nonexamples" to show the nonexamples of scientists. Lead students in a discussion about whether everyone can be a scientist, using the following questions:
   - What does it mean to investigate something?
   - Explain whether you think everyone is a scientist.
   - What makes a scientist a scientist?
   - How do scientists investigate?

10. Explain that the students are going to learn how to become scientists by learning how to "think like a scientist" and by learning about what scientists do. Read aloud *Professor Aesop's the Crow and the Pitcher*. Prior to reading, tell students to look for the scientific investigation processes. Refer to the "What Scientist Do" list. Discuss the following after reading the book:
    - Describe what the crow was investigating.
    - Describe a time when you investigated something.
    - How was the crow like a scientist?
    - How did the crow use the investigation processes?

11. Introduce the Wheel of Scientific Investigation and Reasoning using Handout 1C and relate the elements to the crow's investigation. Explain that the students will learn how to use the wheel to investigate simple machines, force and motion, and compound machines.
12. Have students put on lab coats.
13. Pass out student log books. Explain that scientists often keep notes about their investigations in a log book. Ask students to date the first page and respond to the following prompt:
    - If I was a scientist, I would investigate . . .

Concluding and Extending the Lesson

Concluding Questions and/or Actions

- What would you investigate if you were a scientist?
- Describe how scientists study systems.
- Describe whether you would or would not like to be a scientist.
- What kind of scientist do you think studies force and motion and machines?
- Provide books about various scientists and inventors and about machines and force and motion in the classroom library.
- Introduce an "Invention Center" with computer and Internet access to http://www.livescience.com/inventions.

What to Do at Home

- Ask students to ask their parent or some other adult to respond to the question, "What would you investigate/study/do if you were a scientist?"

Handout 1A

Completed Frayer Model of Vocabulary Development on Scientists

Definition	What Scientists Do . . . (Scientific Investigation Processes)
"a person who studies nature and the physical world by testing, experimenting, and measuring"	• Make observations. • Ask questions. • Learn more. • Design and conduct the experiment. • Create meaning. • Tell others what was found.

Scientists

Examples	Nonexamples
• Astronomers—study the universe (planets, stars, etc.) • Biologists—study living plants and animals • Geologists—study the Earth's layers of soil and rocks (sediments and mineral fossils) • Physicists—study matter and energy	• Entertainers • Poets • Bankers

Handout 1B

Incomplete Frayer Model of Vocabulary Development on Scientists

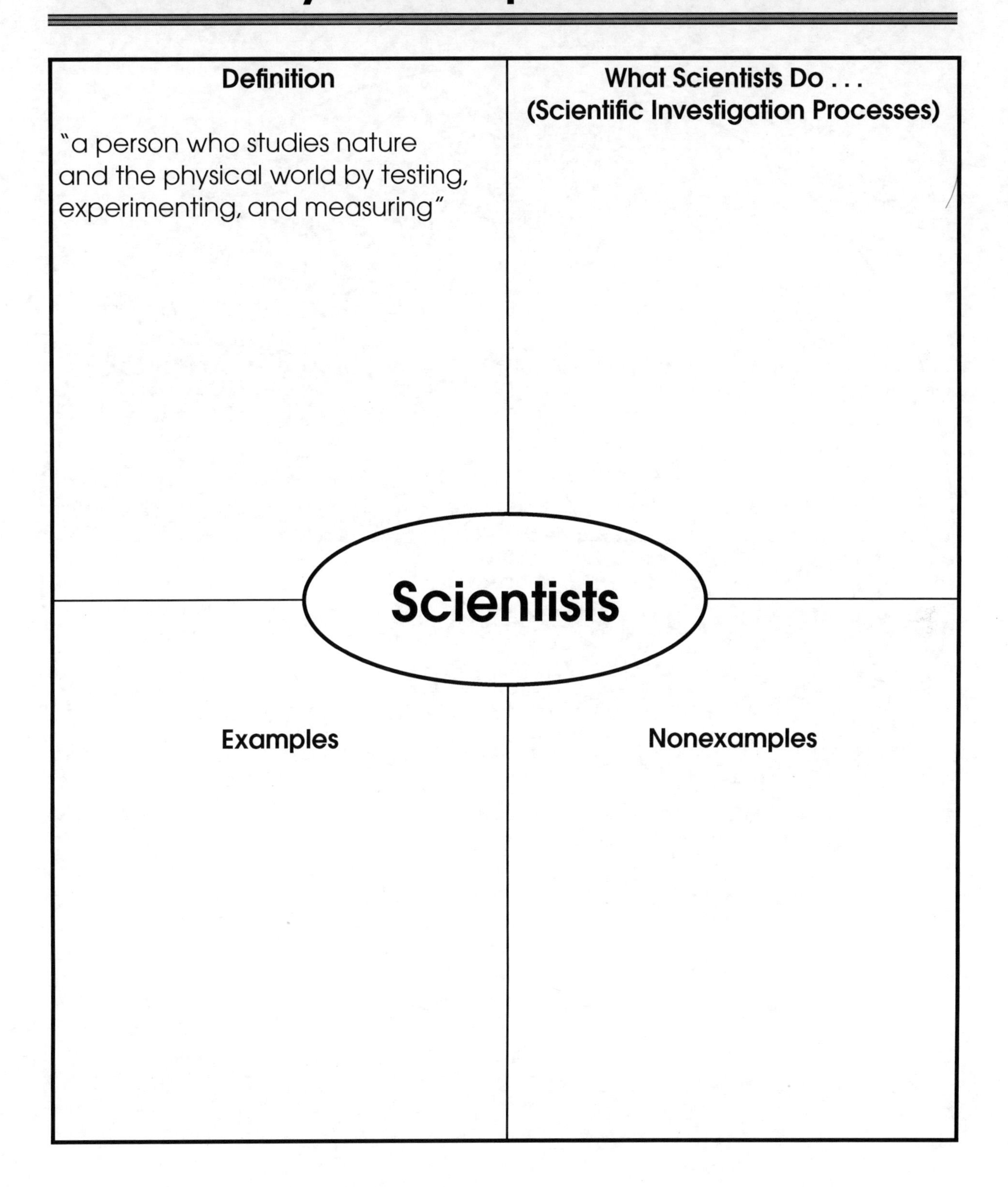

Handout 1C

Wheel of Scientific Investigation and Reasoning

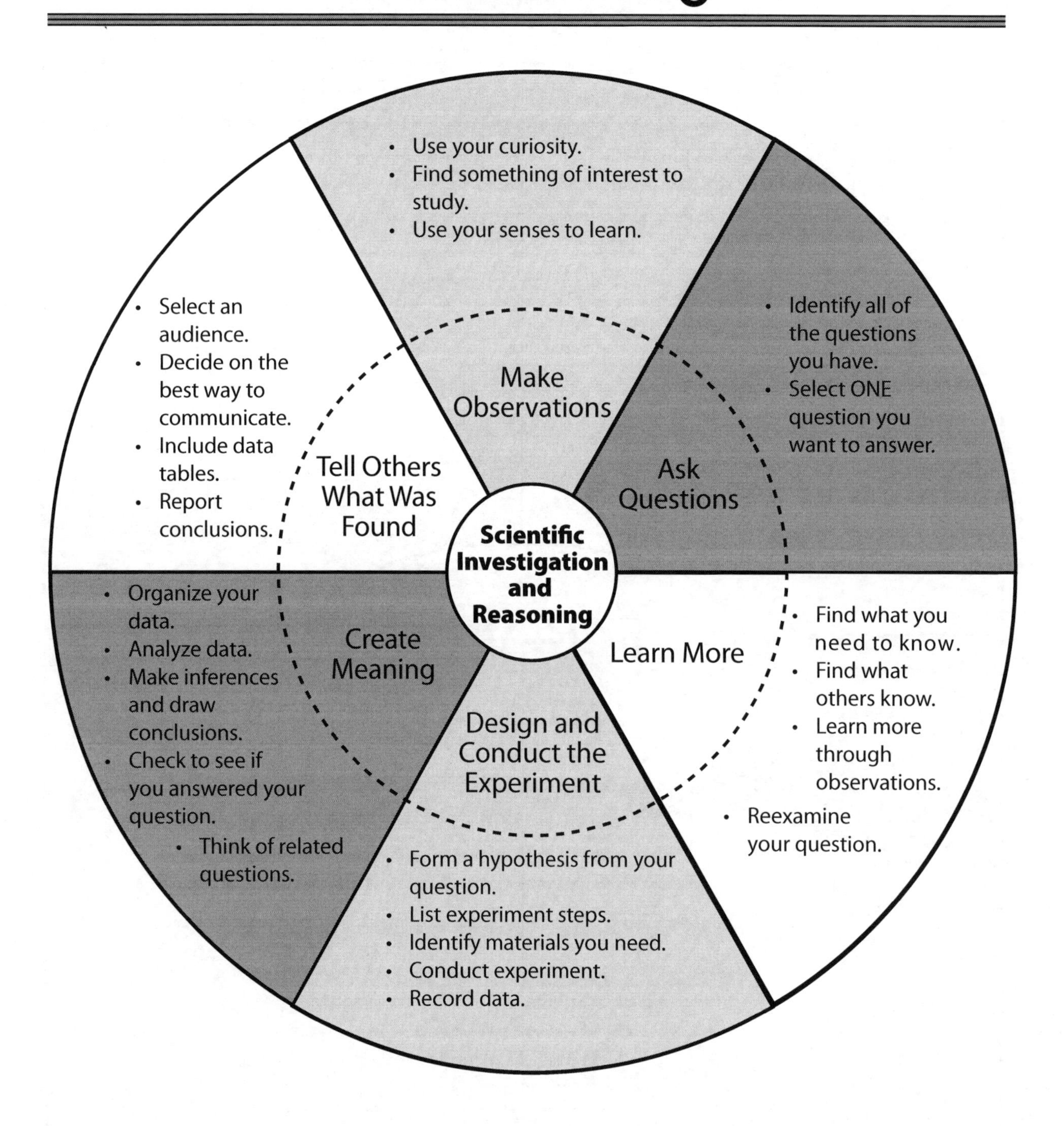

Lesson 2: What Is a System?

Planning the Lesson

Instructional Purpose
- To understand the concept of systems.
- To understand four generalizations of systems.

Instructional Time
- 45 minutes

Systems Concept Generalizations
- Systems have parts (elements).
- Systems have boundaries.
- Systems have inputs and outputs.
- The interactions and outputs of a system change when its inputs, elements, or boundaries change.

Key Science Concepts
- Simple machines are tools that make work easier.
- Compound machines combine two or more simple machines.

Assessment "Look Fors"
- Students can provide examples of systems.
- Students can categorize examples of systems, explaining their reasoning.
- Students show understanding of the concept of "generalization."
- Students can provide an example for a system generalization.
- Students can provide nonexamples of systems.

Materials/Resources/Equipment
- Model of a car
- PowerPoint slides, transparencies, or charts of Handouts 2A (Picture of a Car), 2B (System Definitions), 2C (Car Systems Model), and 2D (Understanding Systems)
- Copies of Handout 2A, one per group of three or four students
- Copies of Handout 2E (Blank Systems Model), one per student

Implementing the Lesson

1. Divide students into groups of three or four. Explain that a functioning car is an example of a system. Pass out copies of Handout 2A to students and allow them to examine a model of a car. Ask students to look at the slide, transparency, or chart of Handout 2A. Have students discuss, draw, and label the parts of a car, what must go into it regularly, and what comes out of the car.
2. Use the chart or overhead as you ask the following questions:
   - What things are parts of the car?
   - What is necessary for a car to move?
   - What must go in?
   - What must come out?

- Are there some things that are essential for your car and some that are optional?

3. Have each group share what it included on its diagram. Begin grouping the ideas that students share on a piece of chart paper to correspond with the categories of things in a system: elements, boundaries, inputs, outputs, and interactions. Ask the following questions to enhance understanding and explain aspects of the system:
   - What are the parts of the car (e.g., the body, wheels, doors, engine, windows, etc.)? All of the things that are part of the car are *elements*.
   - What keeps the elements of the car together (e.g., the sides, top, and bottom of the car)?
   - What are the edges or boundaries of the system (e.g., the top of the car, the bottom, the sides, the tires)? *Boundaries* help us understand where a system begins and what things are inside a system.
   - What are some things that have to be added to the car regularly to keep it moving (e.g., fuel, oil, air, people)? The things that are put into a system to keep it going are called *inputs*.
   - What things come out of the car and its elements (e.g., exhaust, people)? The things that a system produces or lets out are called *outputs*.
   - What are some of the things that happen in the car to use the inputs and produce the outputs (e.g., the engine uses fuel to run; the tires need air to stay inflated)?
   - How do cars use the inputs and give off outputs (e.g., the engine uses the input of fuel to move; people put in a key to start the ignition)? The things that happen in a system to use the inputs and give off the outputs are called *interactions*. Tell students that there are many different kinds of systems. Some systems are small and their boundaries, elements, inputs, outputs, and interactions are easy to see. Other systems are very complex.

4. Share the system's definitions (Handout 2B) and show how they apply (Handout 2C).
5. Discuss the differences between things that are systems and the things that are not. Have students share examples of other things they think are systems and identify the system parts. Then have students identify things that are not systems. Record students' responses on a chart created from Handout 2D.
6. Encourage students to define "system" and support them in concluding that systems have identifiable elements and definable boundaries. Most systems receive input in the form of material or information from outside their boundaries and generate output to the world outside their boundaries.
7. Explain that generalizations are like definitions, but they go beyond definitions by explaining more about how we understand the concept. Explain that they will be learning some generalizations or descriptions that apply to all different kinds of systems. They will be using these generalizations in the upcoming lessons when discussing systems (see Handout 2D).
   - Systems have parts (elements).
   - Systems have boundaries.
   - Systems have inputs and outputs.
   - The interactions and outputs of a system change when its inputs, elements, or boundaries change.

8. Tell students that they are going to be learning about machines during this unit. Explain to students that as they work through this unit, they will be

exploring the concept of systems. They will learn about simple machines and compound machines.

Concluding and Extending the Lesson

Concluding Questions and/or Actions

- Choose one of the generalizations about systems. Write three or more sentences explaining how it applies to another system you know about. Remember to include your reasons or examples to show how the generalization is true. Draw your system example.
- Distribute copies of the Blank Systems Model (Handout 2E). Have students choose a system from the class list of examples and show how it fits into the model. Use a piece of chart paper to post the generalizations about systems on one of the walls in the classroom. Remind students to reference these generalizations in the upcoming lessons when discussing systems. Add to the generalizations with examples from corresponding lessons, using it as a record of examples and observations.

What to Do at Home

- Have students share the generalizations about systems with someone at home. Ask the students to ask that person to give examples and nonexamples of systems and have them explain why they made that determination. Students should be prepared to share with the class!

Handout 2A
Picture of a Car

Handout 2B
System Definitions

Element: a distinct part of the system

Boundary: something that indicates or fixes a limit on the size or spread of a system

Interaction: the nature of connections made between/among elements and inputs of a system

Input: something that is put into the system

Output: something that is produced by the system; a product of the interactions

Handout 2C

Car System Model

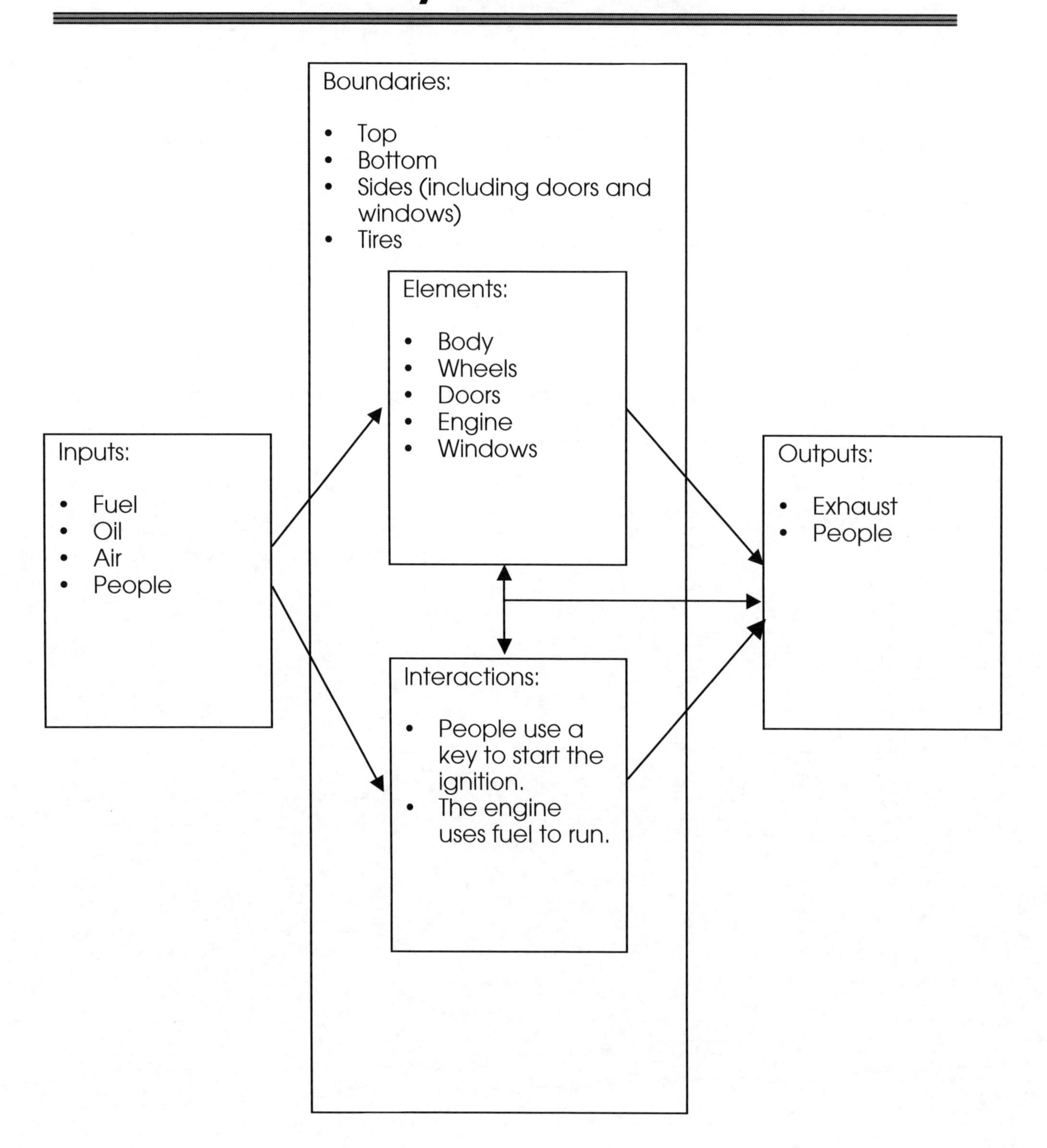

Handout 2D

Understanding Systems

Examples of Systems

Things That Are NOT Systems

Generalizations About Systems

- Systems have parts (elements).
- Systems have boundaries.
- Systems have inputs and outputs.
- The interactions and outputs of a system change when its inputs, elements, or boundaries change.

Name:______________________________ Date:___________

Handout 2E

Blank Systems Model

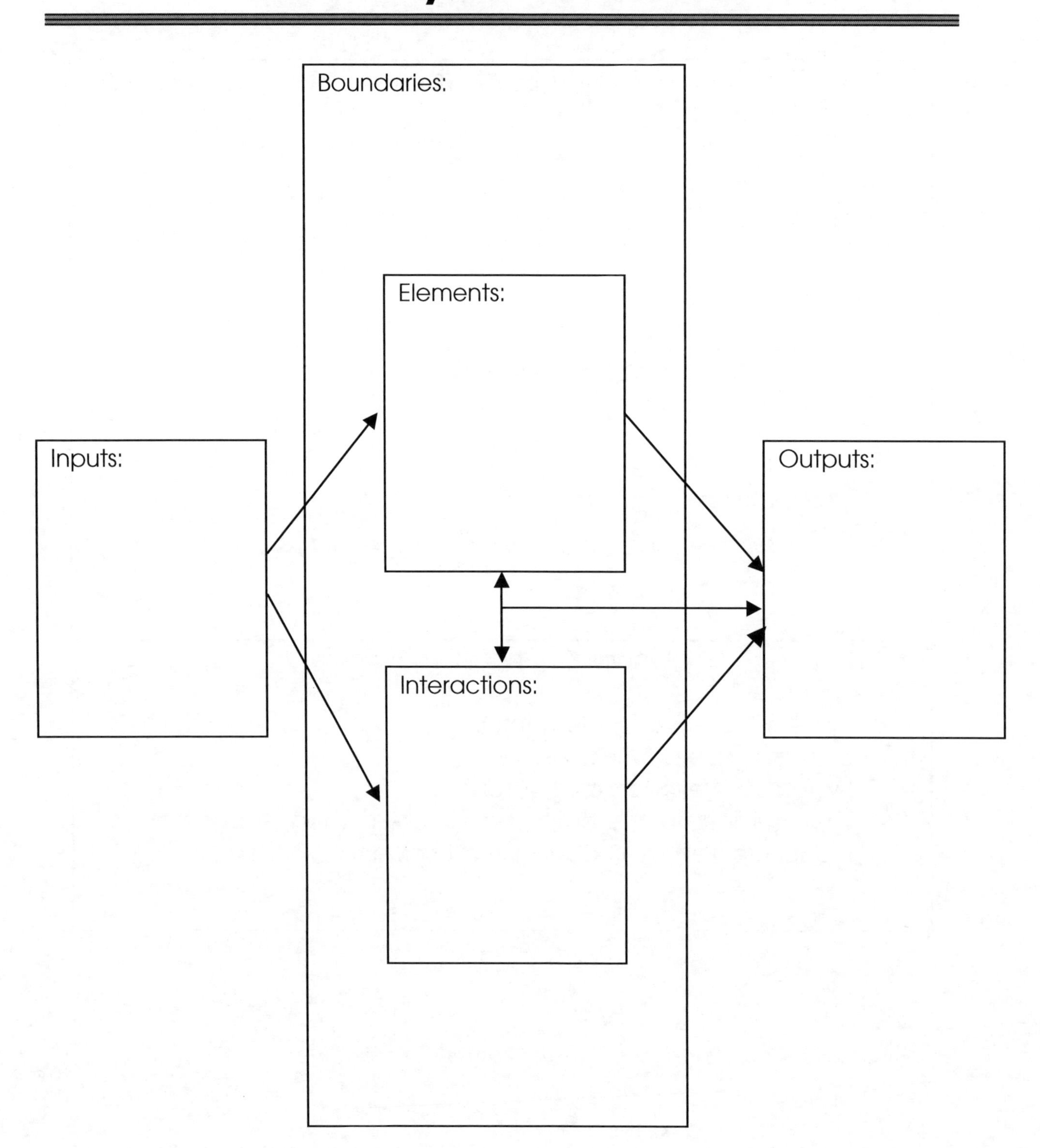

Lesson 3: What Scientists Do—Observe, Question, Learn More

Planning the Lesson

Note to Teacher: The foam board should be half covered in the towel or canvas and should be taped down or secured before class.

Instructional Purpose

- To apply three of six investigation processes (Make Observations, Ask Questions, and Learn More) described in the Wheel of Scientific Investigation and Reasoning.
- To understand force, motion, and friction.

Instructional Time

- 45 minutes

Systems Concept Generalizations

- Systems have parts (elements).
- Systems have boundaries.
- Systems have inputs and outputs.
- The interactions and outputs of a system change when its inputs, elements, or boundaries change.

Key Science Concepts

- Motion is an object's direction and speed.
- Changes in speed or direction are caused by forces.
- Moving objects have kinetic energy.
- Objects capable of kinetic energy due to their position have potential energy.

Scientific Investigation Skills and Processes

- Make observations.
- Ask questions.
- Learn more.

Assessment "Look Fors"

- Students can apply the steps of the scientific process.
- Students can define motion, force, kinetic and potential energy, and friction and state examples.

Materials/Resources/Equipment

- One toy car and one toy truck per group of three or four students
- Charts of Handouts 3A (Wheel of Scientific Investigation and Reasoning) and 3B (Force and Motion Definitions)
- Copies of Handout 3A (one per student)
- Sentence strip with the question, "How does surface type affect speed?"
- Chart paper
- One piece of foam board
- Towel, canvas, or other textured material
- Masking tape

- One ruler
- Student log books

> **Note to Teacher:** Handout 3A should be posted throughout the unit for easy reference.

Implementing the Lesson

1. Have students share their experiences from talking to their family about systems in Lesson 2.
2. Explain to students that they are going to learn to "think like a scientist" and learn how to use the scientific investigation process.
3. Distribute copies of the Wheel of Scientific Investigation and Reasoning (Handout 3A) to all students. Tell students that scientists use these processes when learning about the world. Engage students in a discussion using the following questions:
    - What do scientists do to conduct an experiment?
    - Which part of an investigation do you think would be most difficult? Why?

4. Show students the toy car and the toy truck. Place them on a surface that is easily visible to all students. Explain that they are going to practice thinking like scientists using the Wheel of Scientific Investigation and Reasoning. Direct students to the Make Observations section of the wheel, pointing out that scientists use their senses to learn.
5. Create groups of three or four students and give each group a car and truck. Ask the students to describe the position of the car. Ask the students to share with each other what they wrote. Tell the students to move the car and truck into another position and ask them to describe the position of the truck. Repeat as needed. Explain that it is important to be able to discuss the position of an object. It is an important part of the Make Observations section of the wheel. Questions to ask the students include:
    - Where is the car relative to the truck?
    - Where is the truck relative to the car?
    - Where are the car and/or truck relative to you?

6. Instruct the students to move either the car or truck so that it rolls across the surface. Ask the students:
    - What did you see?
    - Why did it move?

7. Explain to students that this movement is called motion. Motion is an object's direction and speed. Objects in motion have kinetic energy. Ask students to brainstorm other examples of motion that they see every day by asking the questions below. Give them time to generate a list.
    - How many examples did you think of?
    - How many of the examples are systems?
    - Can the examples of motion be put into categories? Is there more than one way to make an object move?

8. Explain to the students that a force is any push or pull that causes an object to move, stop, or change speed or direction. Demonstrate pushing and pulling the car. Question the students about force and motion as you are pushing and pulling the car.
    - What is force? What are some examples?
    - What is motion?

- When will a car have potential energy?
- When will a car have kinetic energy?
- When you make observations, you use your senses to learn. What sense do you use most to make observations?

9. Direct students' attention to the section on the wheel labeled Ask Questions. Ask the students how the car's motion would change, when force is applied, if the car was on another surface. Show the students various ramps with different surface types. Guide the discussion toward the question you have modeled. Model this section by writing down one question you have on the sentence strip that was prepared ahead of time:
   - How does surface type affect speed?

10. Conduct the following demonstration. Place the piece of foam board, prepared ahead of time with the textured material, with several books under it to create a ramp. Use a ruler or yardstick at the top so that the starting time for the cars will be the same. Release the cars down the ramp. Ask the following questions before and after the demonstration (as you ask the questions, have the students write down the questions and their answers in their log books):
    - On which surface did the car move the fastest?
    - Why do you think that happened?

11. Ask students to brainstorm other questions they have about surface type and speed and then write their questions on a large piece of chart paper. Tell the students that they will conduct an experiment in the next lesson to test a new question.
12. Refer to the third section on the wheel labeled Learn More. Ask students what can be done to learn more about something (i.e., Internet research, reading books, speaking with experts), using the following questions as prompts:
    - How can you learn more about something?
    - What do you think is the best way to learn? Why?

13. Point out that one way they can learn more is through additional observations, which will be done in the next lesson through an experiment.
14. Ask students to complete another entry in their log books and date the page. Students should answer the following:
    - When observing the cars, I found . . .
    - How is a car a system?
    - Are other machines systems? What is an example?

Concluding and Extending the Lesson

Concluding Questions and/or Actions

- What kind of experiment might we conduct tomorrow?
- Why would it be helpful for scientists to compare observations?
- Review Handout 3B with the students in preparation for tomorrow.

What to Do at Home

- Ask students to work with their family to observe motion, force, speed, direction, kinetic and potential energy, and friction. Where do they observe examples? Students should compile a list of their observations.

Name:________________________________ Date:____________

Handout 3A

Wheel of Scientific Investigation and Reasoning

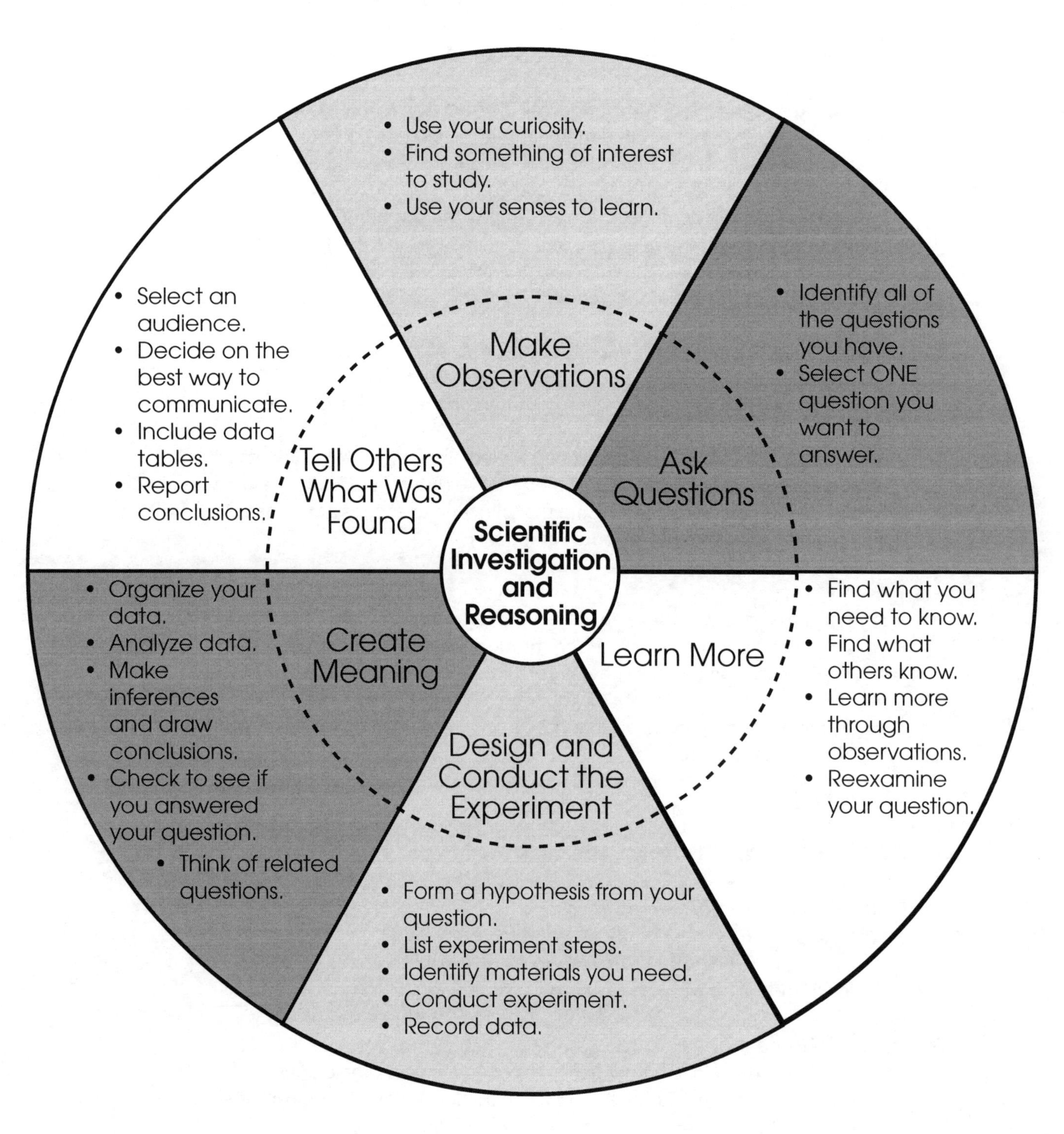

Note. Adapted from Kramer (1987).

Handout 3B

Force and Motion Definitions

- The position of an object can be described by locating it relative to another object or the background.
- Motion is an object's direction and speed.
- Changes in speed or direction of motion are caused by forces.

Lesson 4: What Scientists Do—Experiment, Create Meaning, Tell Others

Planning the Lesson

Note to Teacher: The teacher will need to have the ramps ready before class. One half should be smooth, and the other half should be covered in a coarse material. The rotation the students will take through the stations should be determined prior to the start of class as well.

Instructional Purpose

- To apply three of six investigation processes (Design and Conduct the Experiment, Create Meaning, Tell Others What Was Found) described in the Wheel of Scientific Investigation and Reasoning to design and conduct an experiment about speed, motion, and friction using toy cars.

Instructional Time

- 45 minutes

Systems Concept Generalizations

- Systems have parts (elements).
- Systems have boundaries.
- Systems have inputs and outputs.
- The interactions and outputs of a system change when its inputs, elements, or boundaries change.

Key Science Concepts

- Motion is an object's direction and speed.
- Changes in speed or direction are caused by forces.
- Friction is a force that opposes motion.
- Moving objects have kinetic energy.
- Objects capable of kinetic energy due to their position have potential energy.

Scientific Investigation Skills and Processes

- Make observations.
- Ask questions.
- Learn more.
- Design and conduct the experiment.
- Create meaning.
- Tell others what was found.

Assessment "Look Fors"

- Students can define motion, force, kinetic and potential energy, and friction and state examples.
- Students can apply the steps of the scientific process.
- Students can interpret data from a data table.
- Students can describe how the experiment was conducted and what results were found.

Materials/Resources/Equipment

- PowerPoint slides, transparencies, or charts of Handouts 4A (Road Surfaces), 4B (Definition of Hypothesis), 4C (Using a Question to Form a Hypothesis), 4D (Steps for Friction Experiment), and 4E (Friction Experiment Data Sheet)
- Student copies of Handout 4E
- One badge per student created from Handout 4F (Scientific Investigation Badges)
- Sentence strip with the question, "How does surface type affect speed?"
- Two of the same cars per group of three to four students
- Stations that have: four to five foam-board ramps half smooth and half covered in a textured material (e.g., sandpaper, towel, bubble wrap, carpet). Each station should be set up so that students compare a car's motion down a smooth surface versus a coarse surface.
- 2-inch, 4-inch, and 6-inch blocks of wood at each station
- Yardstick or measuring tape at each station
- One ruler per group of three or four students
- Student log books

Implementing the Lesson

1. Ask students to share their findings from the homework assignment, asking them:
   - What examples of motion, force, speed, direction, kinetic and potential energy, and friction did you observe?

2. Conduct a brief review of yesterday's lesson, using the following questions:
   - What did we investigate yesterday?
   - How did we begin our investigation?
   - What scientific processes did we apply?
   - What did we observe about force, motion, speed, direction, kinetic and potential energy, and friction?
   - What does the surface of the board have to do with how far the car travels?

3. Tell students that they are going to work on a new problem today while working with the Wheel of Scientific Investigation and Reasoning.
4. Tell students they will start where they left off from the previous lesson—that one way they can learn more is through additional observations. Show students the picture of the various road surfaces on Handout 4A. The pictures are of asphalt, concrete paving stones, and cobblestones. Tell them to think about when they ride a bicycle or rollerblade. Engage them in a discussion with the following questions:
   - On which surface would you be able to move the fastest?
   - Which surface is used to pave many of the roadways today?
   - Why is it important to have a smooth roadway? Why not a rough or bumpy roadway?

5. Point to the section on the wheel labeled Ask Questions. Tell students they are going to experiment with the question that they worked with yesterday:
   - How does surface type affect speed?

6. Point to the section on the wheel labeled Design and Conduct the Experiment. Note that the first thing scientists do to conduct an experiment is to form

a hypothesis from their question. Use Handout 4B to define hypothesis as "a prediction that can be tested about how a scientific investigation or experiment will turn out." Use Handout 4C to model your thinking process in turning your original question into a hypothesis.

7. Have students either turn to their partner or talk in small groups about other possible hypotheses that could come from the question; write down the hypotheses on chart paper. Have students discuss the following:
   - What other hypothesis could we form from the original question?
   - How did you come up with this hypothesis?

8. Explain that the hypothesis needs to be tested and to do that we do an experiment. It is important to plan the experiment by listing the steps. Ask students to tell what they think needs to be done to conduct an experiment for the hypothesis. After students share their answers, reveal the list of steps the class is going to follow (see Handout 4D). Point out the list of materials that are needed for the experiment. Have students think about the following:
   - Let's consider our experiment. What things might cause problems with the experiment?

9. Explain that scientists conduct each experiment more than once to make sure that what occurred isn't just a coincidence. Each group is going to take its cars through the stations to test the effect that the type of surface has on speed.
10. Give each student or group of students a copy of Handout 4E. Explain to students how they will rotate through the stations. Make sure that they know to record their observations as they move through the stations.
11. Once the students have completed the stations, bring them back together. Pair the groups together so that the student teams can compare observation notes. Once they have had a chance to debrief, bring them back together. Ask students:
    - Which car usually got down the ramp first?
    - What happened to some of the cars on the coarser surfaces? What happened to some of the cars on the smoother surfaces?
    - How does surface type affect speed?

12. Explain to the students that *friction* is causing the cars to move at different rates. It is a force that opposes motion. Friction causes some of the kinetic energy to turn into heat, but not enough to feel in this experiment. Relate this to the examples used in the beginning of the lesson about the different road surface types. Surfaces that are rough like the cobblestones produce a lot of friction. Surfaces that are smooth like the asphalt produce little friction. Have the students copy the definition of friction and give some examples. In terms of the experiment, ask the students the following questions:
    - Which surface had the least amount of friction?
    - Which surface had the most friction?
    - Which surface allowed the car the most kinetic energy?

13. Tell students that they have just conducted an experiment. They tested their hypothesis, and now they need to do the final two processes: Create Meaning and Tell Others What Was Found.
14. Explain that scientists use charts to organize their data so they can figure out or analyze what the data show—to Create Meaning from the experiment. Ask a reporter from each group to share the group's findings. Use chart paper recreating Handout 4E to record the findings. Tell the students that they are

to come up with an *inference*—a conclusion about whether the prediction or hypothesis was correct. Ask students:
- Was there a difference in the cars' speeds based on the different surfaces?
- What might have caused the difference?
- What do our data tell us?
- Was our hypothesis correct?
- Did we answer our original question?
- What other questions do you have?
- What other experiments in force and motion do you think we could do?

15. Explain that now the class needs to Tell Others What Was Found. Ask student pairs or small groups to decide who they should tell about their experiment findings and how they should communicate their findings. Allow students to share their findings with the whole class and lead them to see that one way they could communicate the results is by sharing the experiment data chart. Ask students:
    - What is important about what we found?
    - How could the information that we found be useful?

16. Proclaim that the students have just conducted a scientific experiment and give out badges saying "I Conducted an Experiment in Science—Ask Me About It!" (Handout 4F). Also, ask students to date and make one of the following entries in their log books:
    - When it comes to conducting scientific investigations, the most difficult thing is . . .
    - The next investigation I would like to conduct on force, motion, speed, or friction is . . .

Concluding and Extending the Lesson

Concluding Questions and/or Actions

- Share student log book entries.
- What do you think we could have changed about the way we did our experiment?
- What can you explain about road surfaces now? Why are they smooth?
- Have the students look at the chart of questions from the previous lesson. Ask them to pick one of the questions and have them write in their log books how they might plan an experiment to test the question.

What to Do at Home

- Have the students work with an adult at home to use the Wheel of Scientific Investigation and Reasoning to conduct an experiment about friction. Ask students to write down the steps to the experiment like this one:
    - Freeze a pan of ice.
    - Roll a toy car across the ice and across another smooth surface.
    - What do you notice?
    - Record your observations and write down any questions you now have.

Handout 4A
Road Surfaces

Handout 4B
Definition of Hypothesis

" . . . a prediction that can be tested about how a scientific investigation or experiment will turn out."

(Scholastic, 1996)

Handout 4C

Using a Question to Form a Hypothesis

My Question:

How does surface type affect speed?

I Learned More:

Friction is a force that opposes motion. A smooth surface has less friction. A rough surface has more friction.

Now I Think:

The type of surface has an impact on how fast an object will move on it.

My Hypothesis:

The car on the smooth side will move faster down the ramp than the car on the rough side.

Handout 4D

Steps for Friction Experiment

Hypothesis: The car on the smooth side will move down the ramp faster than the car on the rough side.

Material Needed:

- Two cars per group of three or four students
- Ramps with a variety of coverings set up at stations
- One ruler per group of three or four students
- Observation forms (Handout 4E)

Experiment Steps:

1. Find two identical cars.
2. Label one of the cars A and the other B. The car that always travels on the smooth surface should be A, and the car that always travels on the rough surface should be B.
3. Place the ramp at your station on a 2-inch, 4-inch, or 6-inch block.
4. Place one car on the smooth side at the starting line and one car on the rough side at the starting line.
5. Hold them in place with a ruler.
6. Release the ruler.
7. Record which car (A = smooth or B = rough) was faster.
8. Repeat steps 4 through 7 two more times before moving onto step 9.
9. Repeat the experiment at the different stations.

Name:____________________________________ Date:_____________

Handout 4E

Friction Experiment Data Sheet

	Car A	Car B
Station 1		
Station 2		
Station 3		
Station 4		
Station 5		

Place a check in the box for the car that arrives down the ramp first.

Our conclusions and questions:

Handout 4F
Science Investigation Badges

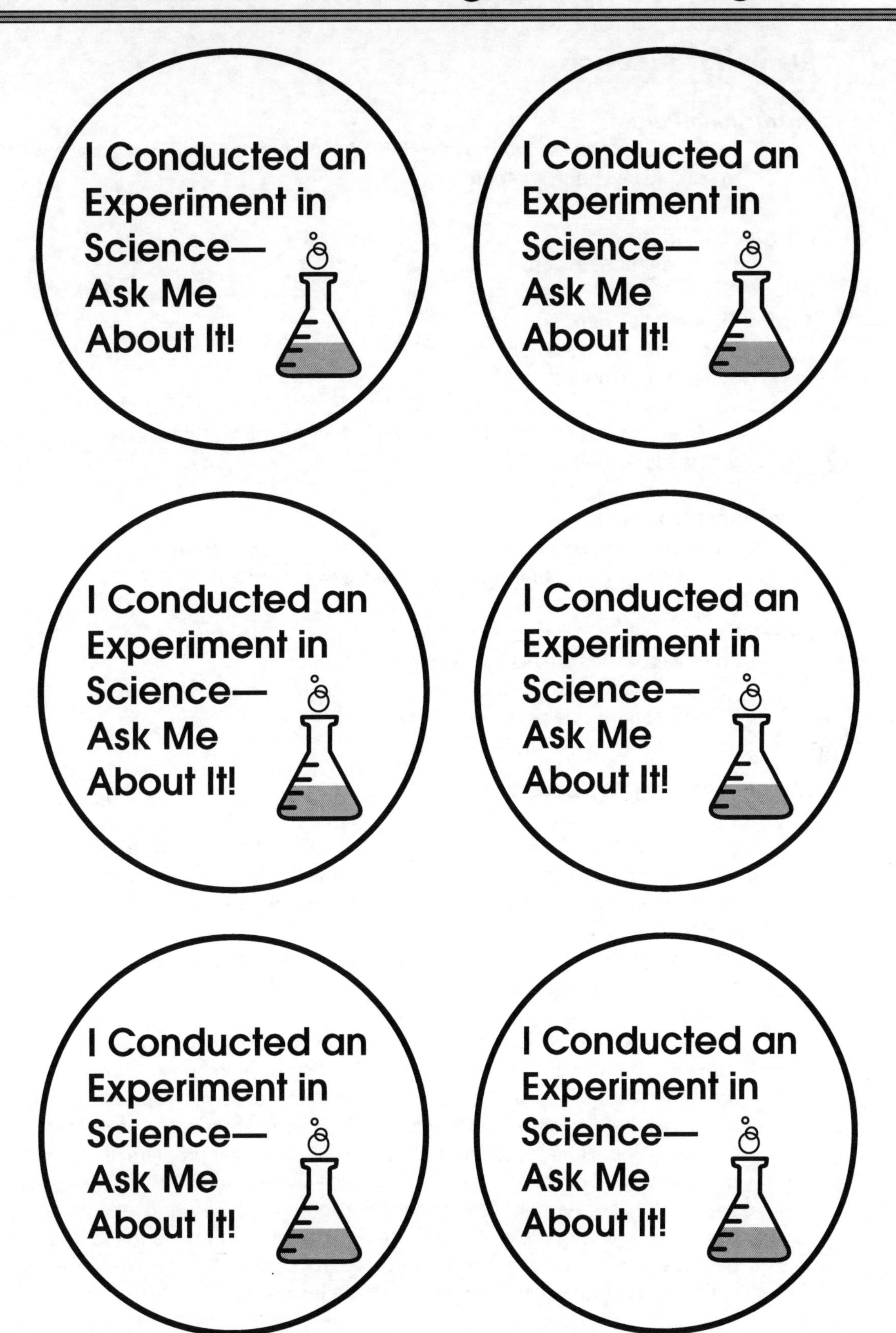

Lesson 5: Creative Problem Solving

Planning the Lesson

Instructional Purpose

- To facilitate students' learning of the creative problem solving process as a way to scaffold invention strategies.

Instructional Time

- Two 45-minute sessions

Systems Concept Generalizations

- Systems have parts (elements).
- Systems have boundaries.
- Systems have inputs and outputs.
- The interactions and outputs of a system change when its inputs, elements, or boundaries change.

Assessment "Look Fors"

- All students understand the creative problem solving process.
- All students can use the creative problem solving process.

Materials

- Chart paper and markers for each group of students
- Copies of Handouts 5A (Problem Scenario), 5B (Exploring the Problem), and 5C (Plan of Action), one per group

Implementing the Lesson

1. Provide a copy of Handout 5A for each student. Ask the students to think about designing something to solve the problem of noise in the cafeteria.
2. In groups of three, have students explore the problem. Give each group a copy of Handout 5B. Ask students:
   - At what times have you encountered the noise in the cafeteria?
   - What are examples of the noise?

   Have students record their ideas in the top section of Handout 5B.
3. Explain to the students that sometimes scientists have to break down a problem into smaller parts in order to think of how to solve the problem. Tell them that these smaller parts to a problem are sometimes called aspects of the problem. Model for the students what might be a smaller problem using one of the examples of noise in the cafeteria, such as the sound of chairs scraping against the floor. Ask the students in their groups to identify and record the top three aspects of the problem in the bottom section of Handout 5B. Then have them select the one that they want to try to solve. Ask them to come up with a testable question that is related to their choice.

4. Explain to students that sometimes scientists try to think of as many different ways as they can to solve a problem, even ideas that may seem silly. This is called brainstorming. Scientists may not use all of their ideas, but brainstorming helps scientists to think about a problem to come up with the best ideas. Based on their testable question, ask students to brainstorm possible solutions to the problem of noise in the cafeteria. Try to get them to come up with as many possible solutions as they can (even silly ones). They should record their solutions on chart paper.
5. Give each group a copy of Handout 5C. In the "Solution finding" section of Handout 5C, ask students to write down the best solutions they have from their brainstorm list. Using these three best solutions, ask students to develop a comprehensive solution based on the best ideas they generated. Explain that a comprehensive solution will use a combination of their best ideas. Students should record their comprehensive solution in the appropriate section of Handout 5C. Questions to ask during the process include:
    - What muffles noise in nature?
    - How would you want to be captured if you were noise?
    - If you could capture noise the way it occurs in nature, how could you use this to create an ideal location for eating in school?

6. Ask students to develop a plan of action to put their solution in place. Students should complete the top section of Handout 5C. Questions to ask during the process include:
    - What needs to be done?
    - In what order?
    - Who can do it?
    - When should it happen?

7. Ask the student groups to share their ideas with the class by posting their papers on the wall and talking the group through their ideas. Question each group in regard to why it selected the statement of the problem and the comprehensive solution it did. Ask other class members to contribute to the ideas shared.
8. Ask students to think about all of the ideas that were presented and ask each group to identify the top solution to the problem of noise in the cafeteria. Students should write the solution that they chose in the "Top solution" section of Handout 5C and then restate the solution as a question. Model a possible question for the students based on one of the students' top solutions. Students should design and label the parts of an ideal location for eating based on their work. Share the designs in the classroom.

Concluding and Extending the Lesson

Concluding Questions and/or Actions

Student reflection: Ask students to think about the process they just completed.

- What parts were easy?
- What parts were hard?
- What criteria did you use to select your best example of noise and to create your comprehensive solution?
- Could you have done the project alone? Why or why not?

Handout 5A
Problem Scenario

You have been appointed the architectural engineer for a new school. Many teachers and students have suggested that cafeteria noise is a major problem in the schools, making it difficult to converse and to think while eating. You have 2 weeks to draw up plans for a cafeteria in the school that would improve on what currently exists in other schools. What will you do?

Handout 5B

Exploring the Problem

Problem: ______________________________

Examples of the problem:

____

____

____

____

____

____

____

Top three aspects of the problem:

1. ______________________________

   ____

   ____

2. ______________________________

   ____

   ____

3. ______________________________

   ____

   ____

Handout 5C

Plan of Action

Tasks	Who	When	Results

Solution finding: ______________________________

____

____

Comprehensive solution: ______________________________

____

____

Top solution: ______________________________

____

____

Restate as a question: ______________________________

____

____

Lesson 6:
The Process of Invention

Planning the Lesson

Instructional Purpose

- To provide support and scaffolding for students to create a new invention.

Instructional Time

- 45 minutes

Systems Concept Generalizations

- Systems have parts (elements).
- Systems have boundaries.
- Systems have inputs and outputs.
- The interactions and outputs of a system change when its inputs, elements, or boundaries change.

Assessment "Look Fors"

- Students can engage successfully in fluency, flexibility, and elaboration of their ideas.
- Students can work in small groups to come up with an original change to the car.

Materials

- Materials for drawing, such as paper, pencils, crayons, markers, or colored pencils

Implementing the Lesson

1. Ask students to describe how they felt when they were working on the noise in the cafeteria problem. What aspects of the work did they find most interesting? Why? Tell them they now will use some of the same processes to come up with their own invention for a problem in the physical world.
2. Show students a model car and ask them in groups of three or four to brainstorm all of the problems that could go wrong with the car. Discuss results and note that brainstorming is a very important part of creating inventions in that it allows you to come up with many ideas in a short time with no constraints on your thinking.
3. Now ask students to think about the car in different ways. How else could the car be used besides driving? Groups should make a list of possible uses. Then, have each group share its list with the class. Now tell them that they have just engaged in flexible thinking—looking at an object and thinking about new ways it could be used.
4. Ask students to extend their thinking about the car to new ways a car might be redesigned to make it more fuel-efficient, more attractive, or more durable. Have them select one of the changes they might wish to make to the car and discuss what could be done. Ask them to draw the redesigned car with the changes in place.

5. After 15 minutes, ask each group to share its drawing and its thinking about the redesign of the car.
   - What ideas do you have about changing the car? Why?
   - What do you need to know to test out your ideas? Where would you go to find out?

Concluding and Extending the Lesson

Concluding Questions and/or Actions

- What are the elements of the redesigned car?
- What are the new inputs?
- What impact do these inputs have on the outputs?
- What interactions are caused by the redesign?
- Tell students that now that they have had some practice in the design and redesign process, they are ready to try their hand individually at invention.

Lesson 7: The Mother of Invention

Planning the Lesson

Instructional Purpose

- To invent a product that will solve a problem encountered in everyday life using the scaffolds provided for research and problem-solving skills.

Instructional Time

- 45 minutes

Systems Concept Generalizations

- Systems have parts (elements).
- Systems have boundaries.
- Systems have inputs and outputs.
- The interactions and outputs of a system change when its inputs, elements, or boundaries change.

Key Science Concepts

- Simple machines are tools that make work easier.
- Compound machines combine two or more simple machines.

Scientific Investigation Skills and Processes

- Ask questions.
- Learn more.

Assessment "Look Fors"

- Students can apply the steps of scientific investigation.

Materials/Resources/Equipment

- PowerPoint slide, transparency, or chart of Handout 7A (My Invention Plans)
- Copies of Handouts 7A, 7B (Brainstorming Form), 7C (Rubric for Invention Creation), and 7D (Problem and Invention Planning Chart), one per student
- T-Chart created on chart paper with headings "Discovery" and "Invention"
- Sentence strip with "'Necessity is the mother of invention'—Plato"
- Sentence strips with definitions of discover and invention
- Student log books
- *Mistakes That Worked* by Charlotte F. Jones

Note to Teacher: This lesson will introduce the students to the final assessment of the unit. One option is for the students to create and build a simple machine to solve a problem. An alternative option is to have the students create a drawing or schematic of what their simple machine would look like. In this option, instead of the students updating their log books with trial-and-error refinements, they will update their logs with the refinements and adjustments they make to their drawings/schematics. The same rubric can be used for this version of the final project, with some minor changes.

For both of these assignments, class time will be needed for the teacher to talk with students about their project and to check progress. An option for this lesson is to allow the students to work on this in class, rather than solely at home. There also is time allotted in Lesson 14 for the students to work on their project. Lesson 14 can be interchanged throughout the unit from this point to allow the students time to work on their projects, or the students can be given the time at the end of the unit after they have obtained an understanding of each type of simple machine. How time for the final project is allotted is at the teacher's discretion.

Implementing the Lesson

1. The *Scholastic Children's Dictionary* defines discover as "to find something" and invent as "to think up and create something new." Engage students in a discussion using the following questions:
   - In your own words:
     - What is a discovery?
     - What is an invention?
     - What is the difference between a discovery and an invention?
   - What are some examples?

   As students supply examples of discoveries and inventions, post them on a T-Chart. If they have trouble, give them the example that electricity was discovered and the light bulb was invented.
2. Ask students what they think the meaning of this saying is: "Necessity is the mother of invention." Read the information about Levi Strauss' invention from the book *Mistakes That Worked.* Additional information can be found at http://www.levistrauss.com/Downloads/History_Levi_Strauss_Biography.pdf. Ask students how this story fits the saying. Then, share the information about George de Mestral and Velcro® from the book, *Mistakes That Worked.* Ask students:
   - Was his contribution a discovery, an invention, or both? Why?

3. Tell students that Levi Strauss solved a problem. Pockets would tear on work pants, and the rivets reinforced the pockets, keeping them from fraying. George de Mestral invented Velcro® after observing how cockleburs adhered to his clothing and his dog's fur. He wanted to understand why and created a product that is widely used today. Have the students name some products that fasten with Velcro®.
4. Distribute copies of Handouts 7A and 7B to each student. Divide the class into groups of three or four for brainstorming. Tell them that because "Necessity is the mother of invention" their job is to think of a problem that they encounter in everyday life and develop a solution. Give them an example like a chalk holder. When teachers hold chalk, they get chalk dust all over their fingers. Someone found a solution to this problem by developing a chalk holder, something to keep the chalk from directly touching your fingers. Solutions to problems can be both simple and complex, just like machines. Tell them that they will be learning about the six simple machines and they can use this knowledge to help develop their invention. As they learn about the different machines, they might develop a need to revise their invention process.
5. Explain to the students that, although the inventions will be done independently, you want them to brainstorm in groups because one person's idea may spark a new idea for the rest of them. Allow them time for brainstorming. Engage students in conversation as you move among the groups, asking them questions like:
   - What problem(s) are you trying to solve? It could be a problem you encounter every day, like a chore.
   - How will you go about designing your invention?
   - Would your invention appeal to many people or to just a few?
   - Is your invention a system? Why or why not?

Note to Teacher: Students might need additional copies of Handout 7A as the unit progresses.

6. Direct the students' attention to the Wheel of Scientific Investigation and Reasoning. In their same groups of three or four students, engage them in a discussion asking the following question:
   - How will the Wheel of Scientific Investigation and Reasoning help you solve your problem?
   - Which steps on the wheel will be most important for you during the development of your invention?
   - How will you learn more about your problem and invention?

7. Give each student a copy of Handout 7C. Explain to them that this is the rubric that will be used to score their invention.
8. Give each student a copy of Handout 7D. This handout can be used to help them plan their invention for the final project.

Concluding and Extending the Lesson

Concluding Questions and/or Actions

- In your student log book, describe how your invention is a system.
- Answer the question "Which invention has changed the world the most?" in a persuasive essay.

What to Do at Home

- Ask students to keep a log of possible problems to be solved and inventions to be created on Handout 7A.

Name:______________________________ Date:___________

Handout 7A

My Invention Plans

Problem	
Brainstorming Solutions	
Other Thoughts	
Materials Needed	
Problems With Development	
My Solutions	
New Ideas	
Purpose of My Product	

Name:______________________________ Date:___________

Handout 7B

Brainstorming Form

Select a problem to be solved related to a machine:___________________

____

____

Choose one of the following simple machines to modify in some way:	In what ways might this machine be changed?	How might you best change it to solve your problem?
1. Wedge	______________________	______________________
	______________________	______________________
2. Inclined plane	______________________	______________________
	______________________	______________________
3. Lever	______________________	______________________
	______________________	______________________
4. Pulley	______________________	______________________
	______________________	______________________
5. Wheel	______________________	______________________
	______________________	______________________
6. Screw	______________________	______________________
	______________________	______________________

Name:______________________________ Date:___________

Handout 7C

Rubric for Invention Creation

CATEGORY	4	3	2	1
Plan	Plan is neat with clear measurements and labeling for all components.	Plan is neat with clear measurements and labeling for most components.	Plan provides clear measurements and labeling for most components.	Plan does not show measurements clearly or is otherwise inadequately labeled.
Construction Materials	Appropriate materials were selected and creatively modified in ways that made them even better.	Appropriate materials were selected and there was an attempt at creative modification to make them even better.	Appropriate materials were selected.	Inappropriate materials were selected and contributed to a product that performed poorly.
Information Gathering	Accurate information was taken from more than two sources and presented clearly.	Accurate information was taken from two sources and presented clearly.	Accurate information taken from a couple of sources but not systematically.	Information taken from only one source and/or information not accurate.
Scientific Knowledge	Explanations indicate a clear and accurate understanding of scientific principles underlying the construction and modifications, as related to the key science concepts in the unit.	Explanations indicate a mostly accurate understanding of scientific principles underlying the construction and modifications, as related to the key science concepts in the unit.	Explanations indicate a somewhat accurate understanding of scientific principles underlying the construction and modifications, as related to the key science concepts in the unit.	Explanations do not illustrate much understanding of scientific principles underlying the construction and modifications, as related to the key science concepts in the unit.

CATEGORY	4	3	2	1
Modification/ Testing	Clear evidence of troubleshooting, testing, and refinements based on data or scientific principles.	Clear evidence of troubleshooting, testing, and refinements.	Some evidence of troubleshooting, testing, and refinements.	Little evidence of troubleshooting, testing, or refinement.
Student Log Book Content	Log book provides a complete record of planning, construction, testing, modifications, reasons for modifications, and some reflection about the strategies used and the results.	Log book provides a complete record of planning, construction, testing, modifications, and reasons for modifications.	Log book provides quite a bit of detail about planning, construction, testing, modifications, and reasons for modifications.	Log book provides very little detail about several aspects of the planning, construction, and testing process.

Total points possible: 24

Name:______________________________ Date:__________

Handout 7D

Problem and Invention Idea Planning Chart

Problem	Invention

Lesson 8:
Introduction to Simple Machines

Planning the Lesson

Note to Teacher: Reviewing this lesson prior to teaching it is essential. There are several teacher's notes imbedded throughout this lesson.

Instructional Purpose
- To identify that there are six simple machines.
- To investigate the purpose and need for simple machines.

Instructional Time
- 45 minutes

Systems Concept Generalization
- Systems have parts (elements).
- Systems have boundaries.
- Systems have inputs and outputs.

Key Science Concepts
- Simple machines are tools that make work easier.
- There are six different simple machines.

Scientific Investigation Skills and Processes
- Make observations.
- Create meaning.
- Tell others what was found.

Assessment "Look Fors"
- Students can identify various types of simple machines.
- Students can use terms such as parts, boundaries, inputs, and outputs when discussing simple machines.

Materials/Resources/Equipment
- PowerPoint slide or transparency of Handout 3A
- One copy per student of Handout 8A (Simple Machine Scavenger Hunt)
- Copies of a different Rube Goldberg invention drawing for each group
- Several types of screws of various sizes, shapes, and number of threads
- Several examples of inclined planes varying in height and length
- Several examples of pulleys such as fixed, moveable, and block and tackle
- Several examples of wedges such as shims, a picture of an ax, scissors, and a zipper
- Several examples of levers with the fulcrum in various places such as scissors, binder clips, a shovel, and a stapler

Implementing the Lesson

1. Explain to students that they are going to be studying the six types of simple machines in preparation for creating their own simple machine to solve a

problem. Ask the students to brainstorm machines using the questions below. Write down their responses in order to form an initial group definition.

- What is a machine? Are there different types of machines?
- What is a simple machine? What is a complex machine?
- What do these things do? What is their function/purpose?
- Are they systems? How do they relate?
- Do they have elements? Boundaries? Inputs? Outputs?

2. Explain to the students that they will make observations on various objects and pictures that you will give them. They will make inferences and draw conclusions from their observations. Arrange the students into groups of three or four and pass out the examples of simple machines. Give each group of students one or two examples of each type of simple machine. The students will need to answer the following questions:
   - What are these things? Are they simple or complex machines?
   - If they are machines, what are their elements, inputs, outputs, and boundaries?
   - What is their function or purpose? What do they do?
   - Have you seen any of these simple machines used in other places? Were they used in the same way or in different ways?

3. Discuss the students' findings as a class. Guide students to categorize each simple machine into its appropriate category. This can be done by guiding the student responses based upon the simple machines' functions and uses. Then distribute Handout 8A. Tell students to keep Handout 8A in a safe place as they will be using it throughout the course of the unit.
4. Explain that there are six simple machines: screw, wedge, inclined plane, wheel and axle, lever, and pulley. As the class studies each one, students will be asked to write a description of the simple machine and then to go home and find items in their houses that use that simple machine in some way. Explain that you also will set up a simple machine center in the classroom for students to classify different simple machines or conduct additional investigations to help them with their inventions to solve a problem. Additional investigations will be added after each simple machine is studied.
5. Introduce the students to Rube Goldberg and his inventions. Depending on how much time there is, you can give a brief or a detailed explanation of Rube Goldberg. Explain to the students that they will be investigating his inventions through observations. Divide students into new groups and provide each group with a different set of illustrations. Students should each receive a copy of the invention their group is working on. These groups are to become experts on their invention and will need to report their findings to their original groups. Groups should answer the following questions:
   - What is the problem being solved?
   - What simple machines are being used?
   - How are they being used?
   - Does this machine make the work easier or harder?
   - What are the elements, inputs, outputs, and boundaries?

Note to Teacher: You may choose to copy Handout 8A on colored pieces of paper so students will be able to find it more easily.

Note to Teacher: Check your library for *The Best of Rube Goldberg* by Charles Keller or *Rube Goldberg: Inventions!* by Maynard Frank Wolfe. Rube Goldberg's illustrations can be found online at http://www.rubegoldberg.com. Previewing Goldberg's work is highly recommended. Be aware that not all of this material, composed in the early 1900s, is politically correct or age-appropriate.

- Is there a way to change any of the elements, boundaries, or inputs to still obtain the same output?
- What improvements or suggestions would you make to Mr. Goldberg on his invention? Why?

6. Once the students are back in their original groups, ask each of the individual experts to explain their findings to their groups. Encourage group members to ask questions or provide suggestions to the expert.
7. Explain to students that you will place the objects or pictures of objects you've been discussing at the simple machine center in your classroom so they may investigate further and sort the various types of simple machines into categories as they have time or your permission.
8. If time permits, allow students to work on the invention creation project.

Concluding and Extending the Lesson

Concluding Questions and/or Actions

- Ask students to refer to their invention planning papers from Lesson 7.
  - What is the problem you are trying to solve?
  - How might simple or complex machines help you solve your problem? Explain by either drawing or writing your ideas

What to Do at Home

- Explain to students that, for homework, they are going to begin a scavenger hunt for simple machines. Their assignment is to interview their family. They are to ask their family if they use simple machines outside of the house or at work and how they use them. Instruct students to record their answers in the third column of Handout 8A.

Note to Teacher:
Throughout the remainder of this unit you may find the following websites (http://www.edheads.org/activities/simple-Machines and http://teacher.scholastic.com/dirtrep/simple) helpful. These websites provide a lot of background information and additional examples of the types of simple machines. You may choose to use these websites as background information or additional information to use in the simple machine center. You also may provide these websites to students for exploration as an extension of the unit.

Name:________________________________ Date:____________

Handout 8A

Simple Machine Scavenger Hunt

Type of Simple Machine	Description/Purpose	Examples
Screw		
Wedge		
Wheel and Axle		
Inclined Plane		
Lever		
Pulley		
Compound		

Lesson 9:
The Screw and the Wedge

Planning the Lesson

> **Note to Teacher:**
> - Prior to this lesson you will need to find screws and nails of the same length and width.
> - (The following can be done as a teacher demonstration or as a class experiment, if you feel that safety is an issue.) Before the lesson you will need to nail two boards together and screw two separate boards of the same size together. Students will determine which is easier to pry apart using a wedge.
> - You may choose to make a few extra sets of boards so students also may attempt to pry boards apart without a wedge.

Instructional Purpose

- To identify the nature and purpose of the screw and wedge. Emphasis will be placed on identifying the screw and the wedge as two simple machines, including purposes for use.
- To investigate why a screw is better than a nail to hold two pieces of wood together.

Instructional Time

- 45 minutes

Systems Concept Generalizations

- Systems have parts (elements).
- Systems have boundaries.
- Systems have inputs and outputs.

Key Science Concepts

- Simple machines are tools that make work easier.
- There are six different simple machines.

Scientific Investigation Skills and Processes

- Make observations.
- Ask questions.
- Learn more.
- Design and conduct the experiment.
- Create meaning.
- Tell others what was found.

Assessment "Look Fors"

- Students can identify various types of screws as simple machines.
- Students can identify various types of wedges as simple machines.
- Students can use terms such as parts, boundaries, inputs, and outputs when discussing whether a screw or wedge is a system.
- Students can record data correctly as part of an experiment.
- Students can articulate findings from an experiment to other class members.

Materials/Resources/Equipment

- PowerPoint slide or transparency of Handout 3A
- Copies of Handouts 9A (Screw and Wedge Experiment Steps and Hypothesis) and 9B (Screw and Wedge Experiment Data and Conclusion), one per student
- Copy of Handouts 9C (Center Extension for Simple Machines Investigation: Screw and Wedge, Activity 1) and 9D (Center Extension for Simple Machines Investigation: Screw and Wedge, Activity 2) for the simple machines center
- Several types of screws of various sizes, shapes, and number of threads
- Several types of nails with different points

- A wooden wedge for each group of three or four students
- Two boards of the same size nailed together for each group of three or four students, plus one extra set (nails should be the same length and width)
- Two boards of the same size screwed together for each group of three or four students, plus one extra set (screws should be the same length and width)
- Examples of wedges: shims, picture of a sledge hammer, scissors that are slanted like a wedge, a zipper
- (optional) LEGO®, K'nex®, Tinkertoys®, and different-sized cars and wheels for simple machines center

Implementing the Lesson

1. Review the homework assignment from the previous lesson. Ask students to share their interviews with their family. Tell students they will need to keep their homework paper, Handout 8A, nearby. You will be introducing two new simple machines: the screw and the wedge.
2. Tell students that today they are going to be studying two simple machines: the screw and the wedge. Hold up examples of several different screws. Ask students to share instances where they've seen screws being used or when they've used screws. Examples might include lids (e.g., peanut butter, water bottles), screws to hold two pieces of wood together, or when their family hangs pictures on the wall.
3. Tell students that simple machines do not reduce the amount of work but they make work easier. Ask students to discuss with a partner how a screw might make work easier. Allow students about 2 minutes to discuss ideas with their partner. Solicit responses and write them on the board. Students should infer that a screw helps hold different items together. Explain that each screw has a certain number of threads. Give each student or group of students several types of screws and ask them to notice the threads. Ask the following questions:
   - Why do you think threads are an important part of the screw?
   - What do you notice about the different screws? How are they the same? How are they different?
   - Which screw do you think will make work the easiest? Why?
   - How might you design an experiment to find out?
   - Why do you think a screw is labeled as a simple machine?

4. Tell students to write a description of a screw and its purpose in the appropriate column on Handout 8A. A screw is a simple machine used to hold things together.
5. Tell students you are going to show them another example of a simple machine: the wedge. Show students various examples of wedges, including shims from a hardware store, a zipper, wedges from blocks of wood in a child's play set, the edge of scissors, the pointed part of a nail, and a picture of a sledge hammer. Pass the items that are safe to handle around the class. Ask the following questions:
   - What do you notice about the different types of wedges?
   - How have you seen wedges being used at home?
   - What is the purpose of a wedge?
   - How does a wedge use force? Explain your answer.
   - Why do you think the wedge is a simple machine? How might it make work easier?

- Is a wedge a system? If so, what are the parts, boundaries, inputs, and outputs?

6. Explain to students that wedges are almost the opposite of screws. Instead of holding things together, wedges help to separate items. Explain how wedges are used in chopping or splitting wood, for example.
7. Show students various types of nails, some with pointed ends, some with wedged ends, and others with ends that are blunt. Ask students why the edge of a nail might be considered a wedge even though a nail holds things together like a screw. Explain that, in order to insert the nail, the wood or whatever is being nailed has to be separated.
8. Ask students to observe the various types of nails you have displayed. Ask students:
   - Which nail do you think would be the easiest to hammer? How do you know?
   - How could you design an investigation to find out?

9. Refer students back to Handout 8A. Tell them to write a description of the wedge, including its purpose.
10. Display the Wheel of Scientific Investigation and Reasoning (Handout 3A) on an overhead or PowerPoint slide. Point to the section of the wheel labeled Make Observations. Explain to students that they made observations by examining the different types of screws and wedges and figuring out how they were the same or different. Next, point to Ask Questions. Ask students if they have additional questions they might want to know about screws or wedges. Solicit responses and write them on the board. Tell students that, for today, you have a question for them to work on. Write the following question on the board:
    - Which is easier to pry apart, boards that are held together by nails or by screws?

11. Link the question you wrote to similar questions the students may have had. Explain that, for today, they are going to examine the question you posed. However, encourage them to try conducting experiments with their questions at home. Point to the Learn More section of the wheel. Ask students if there is anything they need to know before moving to the experiment.
12. You may choose to conduct this experiment as a demonstration. If you choose to conduct it as an experiment, ensure that you review safety instructions with students about how to work with nails, screws, and boards. Divide students into groups of three or four. Explain to the students that they will now conduct an experiment. Distribute Handouts 9A and 9B to each student. Give each group of students two sets of boards that were prepared prior to the lesson: one set of boards that are screwed together and one set of boards that are nailed together. Then distribute a wooden wedge to each group of students.
13. Outline the experiment steps in Handout 9A and allow students time to conduct the experiment. Tell students to reach consensus on which was the easiest and which was the hardest to pry apart, if there is disagreement. Assist students as needed.
14. Ask students to share their findings. How do their findings compare with other groups? (Students should recognize that it is more difficult to pry apart boards connected with a screw than a nail.) Ask students:
    - Why might it be better to use screws to hold things together?

- Remember what you learned about friction and force. How does the experiment today apply friction and force using a screw and a wedge?
- Do you think there are times when a nail might be better than a screw? Why?
- Do you think the number of threads on a screw matters when securing two items together? Why or why not?
- Is a screw a system? Why or why not? Justify your answer.
- What do you think would have happened if you hadn't use a wedge to pry the boards apart?

15. Hold up another set of blocks of wood that are nailed and screwed together. Try to pry the nailed block of wood apart without using a wedge. Discuss the outcome.
16. Explain to students that you will place the objects or pictures of objects you've been discussing at the simple machine center in your classroom so they may sort the various types of simple machines into categories as they have time. Also, explain to the students that you will be adding several invention problems, focused on the wedge and screw (Handout 9C and 9D), to the center for them to work on. You also may add items to the center such as screwdrivers, plastic knives, forks, key rings, clamps, light bulbs, bottles with lids, and other items for students to sort or investigate. Review safety rules for using these items. Store items in a safe place when students are not working at the center.

Concluding and Extending the Lesson

Concluding Questions and/or Actions

- Ask students to refer to their invention planning papers from Lesson 7.
  - What is the problem you are trying to solve?
  - How might a wedge or screw help you solve your problem? Explain by either drawing or writing your ideas.

What to Do at Home

- Explain to students that, for homework, they are going to begin a scavenger hunt for simple machines. Their assignment is to walk around their home and list as many items as possible that use screws and wedges. Examples might include screw tops on various products, wall hangings, tools, and so on. Instruct students to record their answers in the third column of Handout 8A.

Name:________________________________ Date:____________

Handout 9A

Screw and Wedge Experiment Steps and Hypothesis

My question:

Which is easier to pry apart, boards screwed together or boards nailed together?

My hypothesis:

I think boards that are ____________________ together will be easier to pry
(nailed/screwed)

apart because ____.

Materials Needed:

- Two thin blocks of wood nailed together
- Two thin blocks of wood screwed together
- Wooden wedge

Experiment Steps:

1. Use the wedge to pry apart the pieces of wood that are nailed together. How difficult was it to pry apart the nailed pieces of wood with a wedge? Record the amount of time and level of difficulty or effort.
2. Use the same wedge to pry apart the pieces of wood that are screwed together. How difficult was it to pry apart the pieces of wood that were screwed together? Record the amount of time and level of difficulty or effort.
3. Write your conclusion.

Name:______________________________ Date:____________

Handout 9B

Screw and Wedge Experiment Data and Conclusion

My Data:

	Time Taken to Pry Apart (stop after 3 minutes if not apart)	Level of Effort (easy, medium, difficult)
Boards Nailed Together		
Boards Screwed Together		
Other Observations		

My conclusion:

The boards that were ________________ together were easier to pry apart.
(nailed/screwed)

My hypothesis was __________________.
(correct/incorrect)

Explanation:

____

____

____

How do your findings compare with those of other groups in your class? Explain.

____

____

____

Handout 9C

Center Extension for Simple Machines Investigation: Screw and Wedge, Activity 1

Which is easier to use, the same length of screws with more threads or the same length of screws with fewer threads?

Handout 9D

Center Extension for Simple Machines Investigation: Screw and Wedge, Activity 2

Do nails with more wedged or blunt edges go into wood better?

Lesson 10: The Inclined Plane and the Wheel and Axle

Planning the Lesson

Instructional Purpose

- To identify two new simple machines and their purposes: the inclined plane and the wheel and axle.
- To investigate the best height of an inclined plane for a car to travel the farthest.

Instructional Time

- 45 minutes

Systems Concept Generalizations

- The interactions and outputs of a system change when its inputs, elements, or boundaries change.

Key Science Concepts

- Simple machines are tools that make work easier.
- There are six different simple machines.
- Motion is an object's direction and speed.
- Friction is a force that opposes motion
- Moving objects have kinetic energy.
- Objects capable of kinetic energy due to their position have potential energy.

Scientific Investigation Skills and Processes

- Make observations.
- Ask questions.
- Learn more.
- Design and conduct the experiment.
- Create meaning.
- Tell others what was found.

Assessment "Look Fors"

- Students can accurately measure and record the distance traveled by the car and the height of the inclined plane.
- Students can accurately use words such as friction, speed, distance, kinetic and potential energy, inclined plane, and wheel and axle in discussion.
- Students can generate ideas or examples of inclined planes and wheels and axles.

Materials/Resources/Equipment

- Handout 8A from previous lesson (student copy, with rows 1 and 2 already completed)
- PowerPoint slide or transparency of Handout 10A (Examples of Inclined Planes)

- Copies of Handout 10B (Making an Inclined Plane for Distance Data Sheet), one per student
- One copy each of Handouts 10C (Center Extension for Simple Machines Investigation: Inclined Plane and Wheel and Axle, Activity 1), 10D (Center Extension for Simple Machines Investigation: Inclined Plane and Wheel and Axle, Activity 2), 10E (Center Extension for Simple Machines Investigation: Inclined Plane and Wheel and Axle, Activity 3), and 10F (Center Extension for Simple Machines Investigation: Inclined Plane and Wheel and Axle, Activity 4) for the simple machines center
- Piece of blank paper
- Scissors
- Pencil
- Eight dowel rods per group of three or four students
- Ruler, tape measure, or yardstick for each group
- Sturdy piece of 12" x 24" cardboard for each group (alternatively, you could use double- or triple-reinforced file folders)
- One toy car per group of three or four students
- Masking tape
- Different-sized wheels, rods, cardboard, ramps, a doorknob for the students to take apart, and other similar materials for the simple machines center
- Rubber bands or a spring weight measure

Implementing the Lesson

1. Review the homework assignment from the previous lesson. Ask students to share their examples of screws and wedges found in their home. Tell students they will need to keep their homework paper, Handout 8A, nearby. You will be introducing two new simple machines: the inclined plane and the wheel and axle.
2. Ask students if they've ever seen a wheelchair ramp. Explain that a ramp is a type of inclined plane. Tell them that an inclined plane is a flat surface that is higher at one end than the other. Ask students if they can think of other examples of inclined planes. When a car is held at the top of an inclined plane, it has potential energy. When a car is traveling down an inclined plane, it has kinetic energy. Tell them that another popular use of inclined planes is when people move to a new home. Ask students if they've ever seen a ramp on the back of a moving truck. Why would people prefer to use a ramp when moving heavy things?
3. Show students an overhead or PowerPoint slide of Handout 10A and outline the various types of inclined planes involved. Ask students the following:
   - What additional types of inclined planes have you noticed in your home or community?
   - How do you think inclined planes make work easier?
   - What is the relationship between the wedge, the screw, and the inclined plane? How are they similar and different in their purpose and description?

4. Explain to students that wedges and screws are actually types of inclined planes but they are still classified as separate simple machines. Students should easily notice how a wedge and an inclined plane are similar. Tell them that a screw also is a twisted inclined plane. To illustrate, take a piece of notebook paper and fold it as shown in Figure 3. Discard the bottom third of the paper. Fold the paper in half along the diagonal. Cut the paper along the

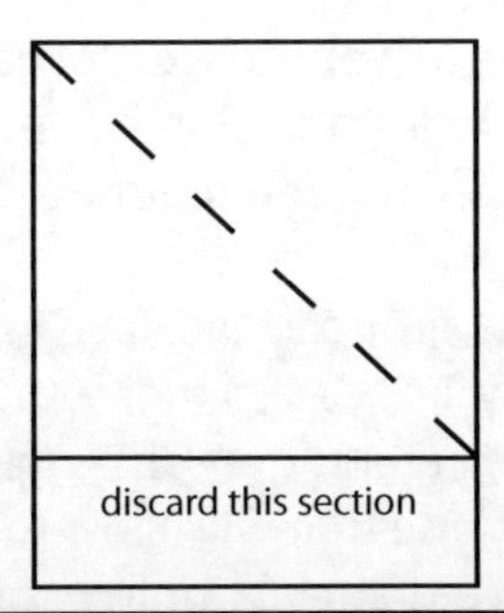

Figure 3. Paper activity for inclined planes.

fold so that you end up with two triangles. Take one of the triangles and hold it up to look like an inclined plane. Take a pencil and hold it up. Begin with the bottom, pointed corner of the paper (inclined plane) and wrap it around the pencil so that the paper overlay looks like "threads" from a screw.

5. Ask students the following:
   - How does this demonstration better explain what you learned in the screw and nail experiment from the previous lesson? Why?

6. Ask students if they've ever driven up the side of a mountain. Ask them if they drove straight up or curved around the mountain. Ask students:
   - Why would road engineers create the road that way?

   Explain that inclined planes are used during road construction, and many times, just like a screw, the inclined plane will gradually wrap around the mountain instead of going straight up or straight down.
7. Explain that wheels and axles are another type of simple machine and are commonly used with inclined planes. Hold up a toy car and identify the wheel and the axle. Explain that axles can be connected as one long rod or separate. If the wheels have separate axles, they can be steered more easily. Vehicles that have one axle have wheels that move together and cannot be steered independently.
8. Tell students to record their definitions and descriptions for inclined planes and wheels and axles in the second column of Handout 8A.
9. Ask students to turn to a partner and brainstorm as many examples as possible for using wheels. Allow at least 2 minutes. Tell students they should have at least 25 examples. Elicit responses and guide students to less obvious ideas (e.g., suitcase, backpack, roller wheels under conveyer belts, winch and cable, well bucket and spool, wringer washer that moves clothes through wheels to dry, old movie projector, earthmover or bulldozer wheels and tracks, pencil sharpener, screwdriver, and doorknob).
10. Tell students to take out a textbook and slide it along the floor. Ask students:
    - How hard do you have to push to get it to move?

11. Divide students into groups of three or four. Give each group of students a set of eight dowel rods. Set the rods on the floor and create a barrier so the rods don't roll away but are able to move freely within a confined space. Slide the same textbook across the rods. What happened? Why? Tell students to explain their answer in terms of friction and speed. Discuss the following:
    - Someone said that wheels are the greatest invention of all time. Do you agree or disagree? Why?

- What is the need for a wheel and axle? What is its purpose?
- What makes it a simple machine?
- Explain that wheels can be used to reduce friction.

12. With students in the same groups, give each group a sturdy piece of cardboard, approximately 12" x 24", a measuring stick or tape measure, and a toy car. Tell students to pretend they are engineers for a stunt driver. They must create an inclined plane that will allow the stunt car to move the longest distance by using the force of gravity only. In other words, they are not allowed to apply any extra force to the car (i.e., no pushing). They must simply let go of the car and measure the distance traveled and the height of the inclined plane. Tell students they may use textbooks to control the height of the inclined plane. Masking tape may be necessary to hold the ramp in place.
13. Distribute copies of Handout 10B so students may record their hypothesis, data, and conclusions. Explain that scientists experiment more than once to verify their findings. Therefore, students should have at least five trials for each height of the inclined plane. Help students begin the investigation.
14. Ask each group to share its data and findings. Compare results. Ask the following:
    - What are the elements and boundaries for the system you created for your experiment?
    - What happens if we change those parts of the system?
    - Do you think the inclined plane could ever be too high? Too low? Explain.
    - What do you think would happen if your stunt car was heavier? Lighter?
    - What do you think would happen if you placed larger wheels on your stunt car? Smaller wheels? (Larger wheels should roll farther than smaller wheels.)
    - Do you think it is important for your stunt car to have one or two axles? Why? What if you were on a racetrack? Would you want one axle or two?
    - Tell students that simple machines make work easier but usually at a cost. What is sacrificed when using an inclined plane? (The distance traveled usually is longer using an inclined plane, but the amount of effort is less.)
    - If someone were in a wheelchair, would you make an inclined plane that was lower and longer or shorter and steeper? Why?
    - What are the interactions and outputs of your inclined plane experiment? How do those outputs change when the height of the inclined plane changes?
    - How do you think inclined planes or wheels and axles might help you solve the problem you are working on for your invention?

15. Add several cars and pieces of cardboard, wooden wheels, rods, and other items to the simple machine center for students to classify simple machines and practice building their own. Also, add the invention problem, focused on the inclined plane and wheel and axle (Handouts 10C, 10D, 10E, and 10F), to the center. Encourage students to work on their inventions.

Concluding and Extending the Lesson

Concluding Questions and/or Actions

- Ask students to respond to the following prompt in their lab books: What are some problems around your house, community, or neighborhood you could solve using a simple machine? Explain?

- Ask students to help you make a list of science words (concepts) that were used in this lesson. Tell students to talk with a partner about these words and what each of them means. Then ask for volunteers to use one of the words in a sentence that talks about something they learned in the lesson. Create a chart of sentences.

What to Do at Home

- Ask students to continue their scavenger hunt using Handout 8A. Tell them:
    - Walk through your home and list items containing inclined planes and wheels and axles. Look beyond the obvious (e.g., car, bike). Let's see who can find the most creative use of an inclined plane and a wheel and axle.
- Have students try the inclined plane experiment at home with different weights of cars or cars with different-sized wheels. Ask students to record their findings and answer the following questions:
    - How are your findings the same or different from the findings in class?
    - What happens if you have carpet?
    - Wood floors?
    - What happens if you extend the length of the inclined plane but keep the same height?
    - Does that make a difference?

Handout 10A

Examples of Inclined Planes

Handout 10B

Making an Inclined Plane for Distance Data Sheet

Height of Inclined Plane	Trial 1 Distance	Trial 2 Distance	Trial 3 Distance	Trial 4 Distance	Trial 5 Distance

My hypothesis:

The higher the inclined plane the ________________ the distance traveled by the stunt car.
(more/less)

My conclusion based on data:

Handout 10C

Center Extension for Simple Machines Investigation: Inclined Plane and Wheel and Axle, Activity 1

How does the distance a car travels on an inclined plane differ if the length of the incline changes but the height stays the same?

Handout 10D

Center Extension for Simple Machines Investigation: Inclined Plane and Wheel and Axle, Activity 2

Is more force necessary to pull a bottle of water up a higher or lower inclined plane? (Hint: Use rubber bands to measure the stretch OR ask your teacher for a spring weight measure.)

Handout 10E

Center Extension for Simple Machines Investigation: Inclined Plane and Wheel and Axle, Activity 3

Do different-sized wheels on a vehicle make a difference to the distance traveled when traveling down the same-sized inclined plane?

Handout 10F

Center Extension for Simple Machines Investigation: Inclined Plane and Wheel and Axle, Activity 4

Do different-sized wheels make a difference to the speed of a car when traveling down the same-sized inclined plane?

Lesson 11: The Lever

Planning the Lesson

Instructional Purpose

- To identify a new simple machine and its purposes: the lever.
- To conduct a simple experiment to determine the best fulcrum and load placement for the easiest lift.

Instructional Time

- 45 minutes

Systems Concept Generalizations

- The interactions and outputs of a system change when its inputs, elements, or boundaries change.

Key Science Concepts

- Simple machines are tools that make work easier.
- There are six different simple machines.
- Changes in speed or direction of motion are caused by forces.

Scientific Investigation Skills and Processes

- Make observations.
- Ask questions.
- Learn more.
- Design and conduct the experiment.
- Create meaning.
- Tell others what was found.

Assessment "Look Fors"

- Students can follow directions to set up a simple experiment.
- Students can measure and record data accurately.
- Students use appropriate science terms such as speed, kinetic and potential energy, motion, lever, and fulcrum.
- Students can draw appropriate conclusions after conducting investigations.
- Students can identify and explain the parts and interactions of a system.

Materials/Resources/Equipment

- Handout 8A, partially completed
- PowerPoint slide or transparency of Handouts 3A and 11A (Examples of Levers)
- Copies of Handouts 11B (Lever Investigation) and 11C (Lever Data Table), one per student
- Lesson 7 handouts for invention planning (Handouts 7A, 7B, 7C, and 7D)
- Two rulers for each pair of students
- Pen with a cap for each pair of students (or a flat-sided pencil)
- Two rolls of pennies for each pair of students (one opened, one closed)
- Masking tape

Implementing the Lesson

1. Review the previous lesson's homework and ask students to identify inclined plane and wheel and axle examples found in their home (Handout 8A). Determine which responses were the most creative or unique uses. Ask students if anyone attempted the inclined plane experiment using a heavier or lighter car or a car with smaller vs. larger wheels. Allow time for students to share their results.
2. Show students an overhead or PowerPoint slide of Handout 11A. Ask them what all of the objects have in common. Allow time for responses. Students should notice that all of the objects lift a load. Explain the definition for lever as follows:
   - A bar that rests on a support called a fulcrum and lifts or moves a load

   Examining the pictures on the overhead, ask students to identify the load and the fulcrum for each item.

3. Tell students to write the definition of a lever on Handout 8A in the appropriate space. Ask students if they know of other examples of levers. Allow time for students to share ideas.
4. Hold up two rolls of pennies. Using a balance or weight, demonstrate that both sets of pennies weigh the same amount. Pose this question to the students: Do you think that you could lift an entire roll of pennies using less than half of a roll? How might this be done?
5. Divide students into pairs. Give each pair two rulers, a pen with a cap or flat-sided pencil to be used as a fulcrum, and two rolls of pennies.
6. Write the following questions on the board:
   - How many pennies does it take to lift a roll of pennies?
   - Where does the fulcrum have to be placed to lift a roll of pennies with the fewest number of pennies?
   - How might you find out?

7. Distribute copies of Handouts 11B and 11C. Remind students of the Wheel of Scientific Investigation and Reasoning (Handout 3A). Place a copy of the wheel on the overhead (or PowerPoint) as a reminder to students. Briefly review the processes for the investigation and instruct students to complete Handouts 11B and 11C with their partner.
8. After students have had time to complete the investigation, ask the following questions:
   - What did you discover about the fulcrum location and lifting a load?
   - Why do you think you had to set the load and the weights on the same mark every time? How might your findings be different if you didn't follow those instructions?
   - How does a lever help make work easier? What is sacrificed to make the work easier?
   - How would you design something to lift a school bus? What principles of design would you use, based on what you've learned about levers? Provide an example.
   - How would a lever help you solve the problem for your invention?
   - How is a lever a system? What happens to the system components when you change the location of the fulcrum?

9. Allow students time to work on their projects for the creation of their simple machine to solve a problem. Direct them to the handouts from Lesson 7 to continue planning. Meet with students as necessary to help them with planning. Students who are further along with their planning of the simple machine invention may work at the simple machine center in the classroom to conduct additional investigations.

Concluding and Extending the Lesson

Concluding Questions and/or Actions

- Refer to the chart of sentences developed in the previous lesson. Ask the students to find the important concept words and to identify the linking words for each sentence. Show them how a sentence would look if it were in a concept map (see Figure 4).

Water is a liquid

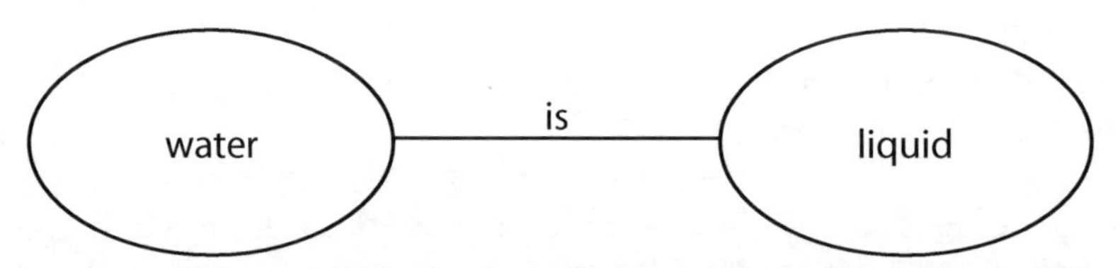

Figure 4. Example of converting a sentence into a concept map.

What to Do at Home

- Have students take home Handout 8A and continue the scavenger hunt for levers in the home. Ask students to be creative and try to find the most unique use of a lever. Encourage students to ask a family member for help.

Handout 11A

Examples of Levers

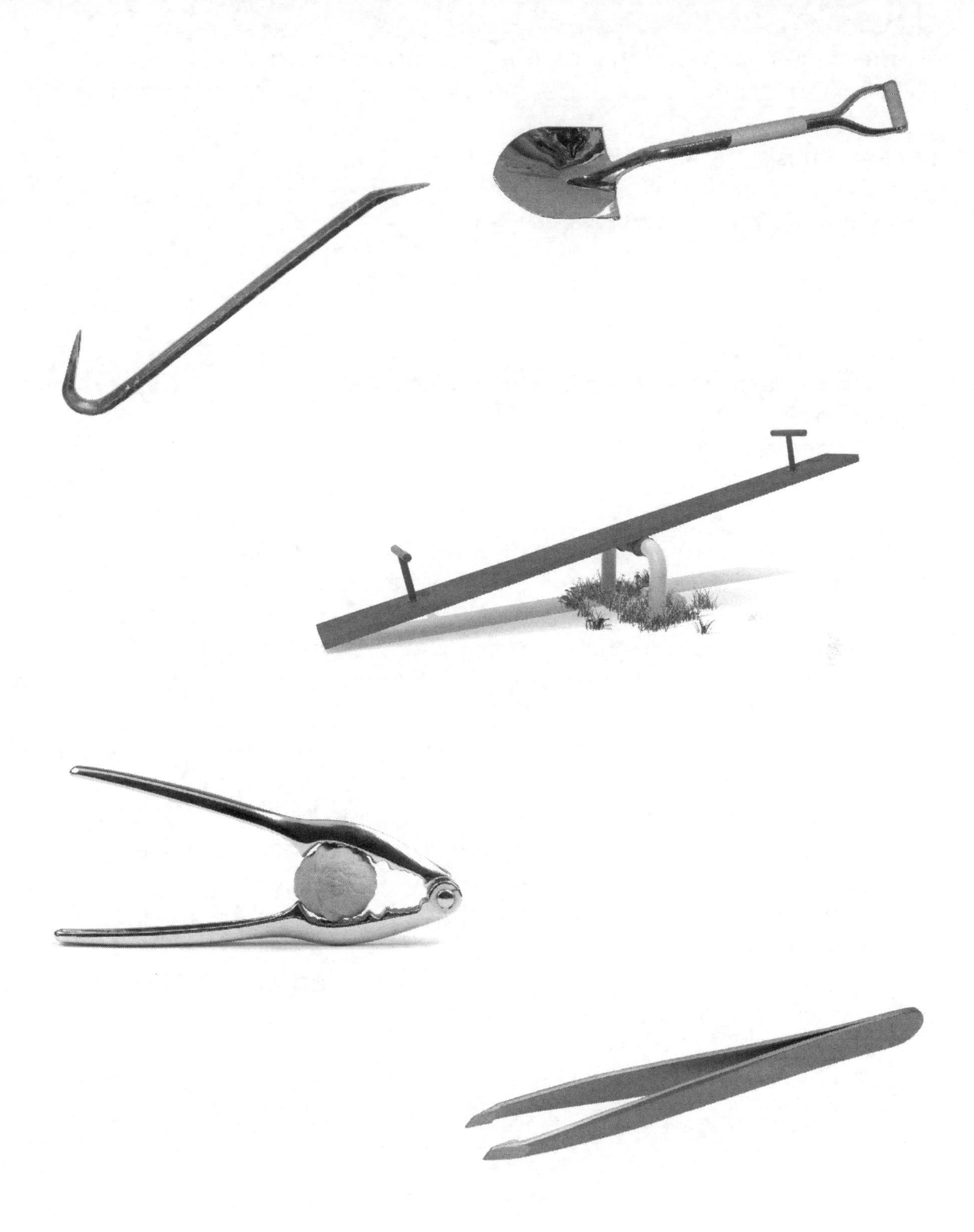

Name:______________________________ Date:__________

Handout 11B
Lever Investigation

Question:
Where is the best location for the fulcrum to lift the most weight?
(What is the least amount of pennies needed to lift a roll of pennies?)

My hypothesis:

I think the fulcrum should be located ________________________
(closer to / farther from)
the load in order to lift the most pennies.

Materials Needed:
- Two rolls of pennies (one opened; one closed)
- Two rulers
- Pencil or pen (fulcrum)

Steps:
1. Place the fulcrum somewhere under the lever (ruler).
2. Place a roll of pennies on the end of the lever as the load. Make sure the roll of pennies remains in the same place for all tests. (You may need to tape the pennies to the ruler to secure them.)
3. Measure the distance between the fulcrum and the load. Record the distance.
4. Open the second roll of pennies. Place pennies one at a time on the opposite end of the lever until the roll of pennies rises. Record the number of pennies. (Hint: Be sure you set the pennies on the same mark on the ruler each time you test. You may need to tape the loose pennies onto the ruler so they will stay.)
5. Move the fulcrum closer to and farther away from the load. Repeat the process.
6. Use the data table to write the conclusion and whether the hypothesis was correct or incorrect.

Name:______________________________ Date:___________

Handout 11C

Lever Data Table

Distance of Load (Roll of Pennies) From the Fulcrum	Number of Pennies Needed to Lift the Load (Roll of Pennies)

My conclusion:

The closer the fulcrum is to the load, the ________________ weight is needed to lift the load.

When using a lever, it takes ______ pennies to lift a roll of pennies.

My hypothesis was _________________ because _____________________

____

____

Lesson 12: The Pulley

Planning the Lesson

Instructional Purpose

- To introduce students to pulleys and how they are used to lift heavy objects.
- To conduct a simple investigation to determine that the more pulleys used, the easier an object is to lift.

Instructional Time

- 45 minutes

Systems Concept Generalizations

- The interactions and outputs of a system change when its inputs, elements, or boundaries change.

Key Science Concepts

- Simple machines are tools that make work easier.
- There are six different simple machines.
- Motion is an object's direction and speed.
- Changes in speed or direction of motion are caused by forces.
- Friction is a force that opposes motion.
- Moving objects have kinetic energy.
- Objects capable of kinetic energy due to their position have potential energy.

Scientific Investigation Skills and Processes

- Make observations.
- Ask questions.
- Learn more.
- Design and conduct the experiment.
- Create meaning.
- Tell others what was found.

Assessment "Look Fors"

- Students can follow directions to make a pulley.
- Students can explain the difference between the types of pulleys and their benefits.
- Students recognize friction in using pulleys.
- Students can articulate the benefits and drawbacks of using pulleys.
- Students can define motion, force, kinetic and potential energy, and friction and state examples.

Materials/Resources/Equipment

- Different types of pulleys purchased from a hardware store, including single and block-and-tackle pulleys
- 2" x 36" PVC pipe or dowel rods for each group of three or four students
- One gallon-size paint can or a gallon water jug filled with liquid for each group of three or four students (must have a handle to tie a rope around)

- 15 feet of ¾" or larger rope for each group of three or four students
- Copy of Handout 12A (Center Extension for Simple Machines Investigation: Pulleys) for the simple machines center

Implementing the Lesson

1. Ask students to retrieve Handout 8A to review their homework assignment. Review the scavenger hunt assignment from the previous lesson. Ask students what additional examples of levers they found. Which was the most creative use of a lever?
2. Tell students they are going to study another simple machine: a pulley. Explain that a pulley is like a wheel and axle but instead of a wheel rotating on an axle, it rotates on a rope, string, or cord. Pulleys are used to raise and lower heavy things. Explain that curtain rods, cranes, and flagpole mechanisms are some common uses of pulleys. Ask students if they can think of other places they've seen pulleys. Write their examples on the board. Instruct students to write their description and purpose of a pulley on Handout 8A in the appropriate column.
3. Explain to students that there are several types of pulleys, including fixed, moveable, and combined pulleys. Pass around different types of pulleys purchased from a hardware store for students to observe. Explain that they may choose to purchase pulleys for their invention if necessary or make their own. Tell students: "You will make your own fixed and moveable pulleys today."
4. Divide students into groups of three or four. Give each group of students a paint can or water jug, 15 feet of rope, and a dowel rod or plastic pipe. Instruct students to do the following:
   - Place your dowel rod or pipe on top of two desks so that it looks like a mini chin-up bar. You may need to set books or other barriers on both sides of the rod so that it does not roll away.
   - Tie one end of the rope to the handle of the paint can or water jug. Loop the other end of the rope across the top of the bar (see Figure 5). Pull on the end of the rope that is not attached to the can or jug and lift it.

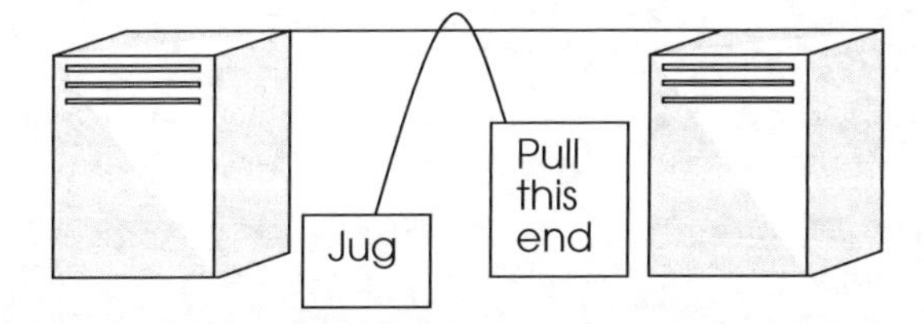

Figure 5. Setup for fixed pulley experiment.

   - Ask students how difficult it was to lift the jug by pulling the rope. Discuss. Explain to students that it requires the same effort to lift the load with a fixed pulley as without.
   - Next, show students how to make a moveable pulley. Students do this by untying the rope from the paint can or jug handle. Instead they tie one end of the rope to the bar and loop the other end of the rope through the handle of the load (paint can or jug). Next, they loop the rope over the bar again and pull (see Figure 6).
   - Allow time for students to pull on the rope. Explain that this is a moveable pulley. Ask students the following:
     - When might a moveable pulley be better to use? Why?

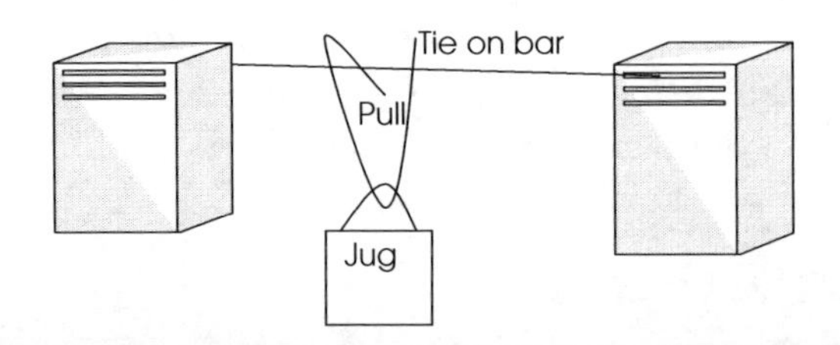

Figure 6. Setup for moveable pulley experiment.

- o When might a single or fixed pulley be better? Why?
- o What would happen if you looped the rope through the handle and around the bar one more time? Two more times? What happens? Try it. (Allow time for students to practice adding more pulleys to share the load.) When might this type of a pulley be beneficial?
- o Even though you must use less force with multiple pulleys, what are you sacrificing? (distance traveled)
- o What would happen if we used a rougher bar to pull the rope over? A smoother bar? Explain your answer in terms of friction.
- o What happens to the system when you change from a fixed to a moveable pulley? Explain.
- o How might pulleys help you solve the problem you are working on for your invention?

5. Explain to students that you are going to place the objects they have been using in the simple machine center for more practice. Also add the invention problems focused on the inclined plane and wheel and axle (Handout 12A) to the center.
6. Allow time as necessary for students to continue working on their inventions. Meet with students as needed. Help them set a timeline for completion.

Concluding and Extending the Lesson

Concluding Questions and/or Actions

- In their log books, ask students to respond to the following prompt:
  - o Now that you've studied the six simple machines, which machine do you think helps humans the most? Why? Justify your answer using specific examples.

- Select six to eight key concepts that relate to this lesson. Copy a sheet that contains these words in large print so that students can cut them up to make a set of cards. Direct students to work with a partner to cut up the cards and then to select pairs of words to make a connection between the words (proposition). Ask students to write their connecting word(s) on small slips of paper and actually connect the cards (see Figure 7). Encourage students to then take another word and see if they can make a connection to the first two cards.

What to Do at Home

- Encourage students to look up the following website to learn more about pulleys: http://www.the-office.com/summerlift/pulleybasics.htm. Ask students to explain to their families what they have learned.
- Encourage students to continue their scavenger hunt at home with pulleys, using Handout 8A. Ask them to find uses of compound machines and record

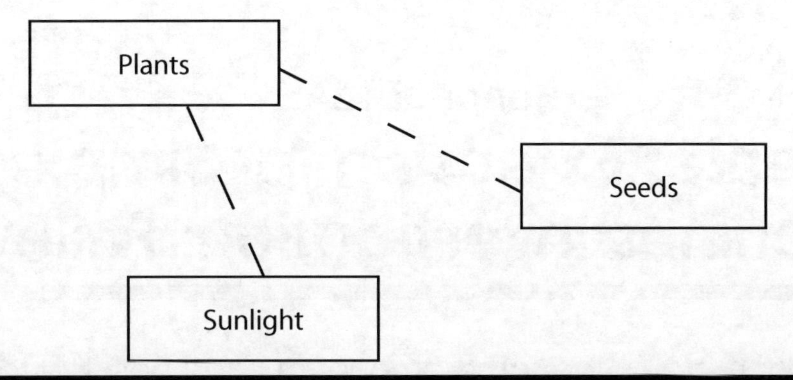

Figure 7. Sample connection of one card (plants) with others.

those in the appropriate column. Remind students that compound machines are more than one simple machine combined—this may mean that more than one of the same type of simple machine is used (e.g., a car that has four wheels) or a combination of two or more simple machines is used (e.g., a wedge and a lever, as in scissors). Challenge students to see if they can find at least 15 compound machines at home.

Handout 12A

Center Extension for Simple Machines Investigation: Pulleys

Is there less, more, or the same amount of effort needed to lift a bottle of water with a fixed pulley? (Hint: Try to balance two jugs of water of the same weight using a fixed pulley. Then try to balance two jugs of water using a moveable pulley. What happens? Why?)

Lesson 13: Compound Machines

Planning the Lesson

Instructional Purpose

- To identify how the six machines may be combined to create compound machines.
- To solve a given scenario problem using a simple or compound machine as a solution.

Instructional Time

- 45–60 minutes

Systems Concept Generalizations

- Systems have parts (elements).
- Systems have boundaries.
- Systems have inputs and outputs.

Key Science Concepts

- Simple machines are tools that make work easier.
- There are six different simple machines.
- Motion is an object's direction and speed.
- Changes in speed or direction of motion are caused by forces.
- Friction is a force that opposes motion.
- Moving objects have kinetic energy.
- Objects capable of kinetic energy due to their position have potential energy.

Scientific Investigation Skills and Processes

- Make observations.
- Ask questions.
- Learn more.
- Design and conduct the experiment.
- Create meaning.
- Tell others what was found.

Assessment "Look Fors"

- Students can quickly identify which simple machines or combinations of simple machines may be needed to make work easier.
- Students can articulate and demonstrate how they would use a simple or compound machine.

Materials/Resources/Equipment

- Handout 8A, completed
- PowerPoint slide or transparency of Handout 13A (Examples of Compound Machines)
- Handout 13B (Scenarios for Building Machines), with each scenario cut out for the students

- Copies of Handouts 13C (Center Extension for Simple Machines Investigation: Complex Machines, Activity 1) and 13D (Center Extension for Simple Machines Investigation: Complex Machines, Activity 2) for the simple machines center
- Materials from the simple machines center
- Additional building or drawing materials, including pipe cleaners, blank paper, markers, scissors, rope or string, wood sticks or blocks of wood, cardboard of various lengths, and other similar materials

Implementing the Lesson

1. Ask students to look at Handout 8A. What types of items around their house did they find that incorporate pulleys? What do they think compound machines are? Allow time for students to share their ideas. Write their examples of compound machines on the board.
2. Instruct students to write the purpose and description of compound machines on Handout 8A as follows:
   - Compound machines consist of the same or different simple machines that are combined to solve a problem or make work easier.

3. Show Handout 13A on the overhead or a PowerPoint slide. Ask students to identify the simple machines used within the compound machines. Ask students to look on the board at the other ideas of compound machines they found around their home. Ask students:
   - Do you have additional ideas of compound machines used?

4. Tell students that now that they have a better knowledge base of simple machines and compound machines you want them to put their knowledge to the test.
5. Write the following statement on the board: "Necessity is the mother of invention." Ask students to recall what that means. Tell them you are going to practice that idea using compound machines.
6. Divide students into six groups. Give each group a scenario written or glued on an index card from Handout 13B. Explain to students that they should solve the problem using at least two simple machines. They may solve the problem with the same two simple machines or as many different simple machines as possible. They must be prepared to share their solution by the end of class. They will have 30 minutes to work on their solution.
7. Explain that students have several options for displaying their solution. They may:
   - Draw a diagram of their problem on paper and explain to the class how it would work.
   - Make their machine using materials from the simple machines center or other materials around the classroom.
   - Pretend they are the different parts of the machine they are making and explain their role in solving the problem.

   Other ideas may be accepted. If students are not sure what they can do, encourage them to ask.
8. Remind students when they have about 8 minutes left and then again when they have 4 minutes left.
9. Allow students 3 minutes to share their solutions.
10. Review as follows:

- Which machines did you use?
- How did the machines you selected make work easier, given your scenario? What was sacrificed?
- What are the parts of your simple machine? How do each work as a system?
- What might be some of the drawbacks to combining simple machines? What are some of the advantages?

11. Explain to students that they will have time in class to complete their inventions during the next science lesson. Instruct them to bring in materials to work on their products as well as additional questions they might have.
12. Explain to students that you are going to place the objects they have been using in the simple machines center for more practice. Add the invention problems focused on compound machines (Handouts 13C and 13D) to the center.

Concluding and Extending the Lesson

Concluding Questions and/or Actions

- In their log books, ask students to respond to the following prompt:
    - Look at the concept words (the unit vocabulary words assembled by the teacher). Based on the machine you built today, how would you link at least six of the words? Draw or write your response.

What to Do at Home

- Have the students talk to their family about their problem and invention ideas and problem. Encourage students to ask their family for additional ideas as necessary. Tell students that they should be prepared to finish working on their invention during the next science lesson.

Handout 13A

Examples of Compound Machines

Name:______________________________ Date:__________

Handout 13B

Scenarios for Building Machines

1. Amira hates to wear socks to bed. However, when she wakes up in the mornings her feet are cold and she doesn't want to get out of bed. Create a machine that will help Amira put on her socks without getting out of bed or out from underneath her blanket until she is warm.

2. Malakai's dad is painting his house. Malakai is helping. However, Malakai spends too much time climbing up and down the ladder handing his dad tools and paint. Create a machine that will help Malakai and his dad solve their problem so Malakai doesn't have to keep climbing up the ladder.

3. Sam's dog, Mr. Chewy, is too heavy for Sam to lift into the bathtub for a bath. Mr. Chewy hates baths, so Sam can't coax him into the tub on his own. Create a machine that will help Sam get Mr. Chewy into the bathtub.

4. Debbie is in a wheelchair. Her favorite sport is basketball. She isn't tall enough or strong enough to shoot the ball into the hoop on her own. The basketball hoops cannot be lowered. Create a machine that will help Debbie shoot a ball for distance and height. It must be easy to operate.

5. Jasmine has several pictures on the wall, but they keep falling down every time she opens her bedroom door. Create a device that will help Jasmine keep pictures on her wall. How might you incorporate at least two simple machines?

6. Jose's mom puts his socks on top of the dryer to fold. Last week she accidentally bumped into the dryer and several socks fell behind the dryer. The dryer is too heavy to move. How can Jose's mom retrieve the socks without moving the dryer? Create a device to help her.

Handout 13C

Center Extension for Simple Machines Investigation: Complex Machines, Activity 1

Sort and classify the different types of pictures or objects into the six types of simple machines or compound machines. Write at least two general statements about each category of simple machines.

Handout 13D

Center Extension for Simple Machines Investigation: Complex Machines, Activity 2

Analyze the six types of simple machines or compound machines in terms of their inputs, outputs, and boundaries. Write at least three statements/inferences about each category of simple machines.

Lesson 14: Final Touches

Planning the Lesson

Note to Teacher: Lesson 14 can be taught in 1–5 days, depending on how much time you want to give the students to work on their inventions in class. Refer to Lesson 5 if needed.

Instructional Purpose

- To finalize their inventions in preparation for their invention presentation.

Instructional Time

- 45 minutes

Systems Concept Generalizations

- Systems have parts (elements).
- Systems have boundaries.
- Systems have inputs and outputs.
- The interactions and outputs of a system change when its inputs, elements, or boundaries change.

Key Science Concepts

- Simple machines are tools that make work easier.
- There are six different simple machines.
- Compound machines combine two or more simple machines.
- Motion is an object's direction and speed.
- Changes in speed or direction of motion are caused by forces.
- Friction is a force that opposes motion.
- Moving objects have kinetic energy.
- Objects capable of kinetic energy due to their position have potential energy.

Scientific Investigation Skills and Processes

- Create meaning.

Assessment "Look Fors"

- Students can define motion, force, kinetic and potential energy, and friction and state examples.
- Students can apply the steps of the scientific process.
- Students can explain their invention.

Materials/Resources/Equipment

- PowerPoint slide, transparency, or chart of the Wheel of Scientific Investigation and Reasoning (Handout 3A)
- Copies of Handout 14A (My Invention Presentation Form), one per student
- Student log books

Implementing the Lesson

1. Give students a copy of Handout 14A. Explain to them that they should work on their presentation while they are finishing up the work on their inventions.

Once they have finished all of the fine-tuning on their inventions, they must be prepared to share their work. Point to the section of the Wheel of Scientific Investigation and Reasoning labeled Tell Others What Was Found. Engage students in a brief discussion about "telling others" using the following questions as a guide:

- Why do you think it is important to tell others about your work?
- How do scientists generally tell others?

2. As you release students to work on finishing up their inventions and to prepare for their presentation, remind them that they should be using the Wheel of Scientific Investigation and Reasoning (Handout 3A). You should circulate among the students, engaging them in dialogue about their inventions with the following questions:
    - What steps on the wheel did you use?
    - What problems did you encounter that you have had to overcome?
    - How is your invention helpful?
    - What simple machines are included in your invention?

Concluding and Extending the Lesson

Concluding Questions and/or Actions

- Compare Handout 7A with Handout 14A. What similarities did you see? What differences did you find?
- Does your invention require motion? Force?
- Is there friction? What impact does this have on your invention?
- Refer to the master concept map for this unit and ask students to find the part on the map that connects to this lesson.

What to Do at Home

- Tell students that they should practice their invention presentation for their family.

Name:______________________________ Date:__________

Handout 14A

My Invention Presentation Form

My problem was ______________________________

____

My invention is called______________________________

____

(Show your audience how your invention works.)

I think people would be interested in this invention because______________

____

____

The simple machines included in my invention are ______________________

____

____

My invention is a system.

1. It has these parts______________________________
   (Point out the parts to your audience.)
2. My invention's boundaries are ______________________________
   (Point out the boundaries to your audience.)
3. My invention has these inputs and outputs______________________

   ____

   (Point out the inputs and outputs.)
4. The interactions of my system are ______________________________

   ____

(Ask your audience if they have any questions.)

Lesson 15:
Invention Fair

Planning the Lesson

> **Note to Teacher:** This lesson combines the presentation of the students' inventions and the review of the unit. The intention here is for the students to make the connection between their own inventions and their classmates' inventions to the macroconcepts and key science concepts in the unit.

Instructional Purpose
- To do the invention presentation.
- To begin to review the unit principles, including key science concepts and concept generalizations.

Instructional Time
- One to three 45-minute lessons, depending on class size

Systems Concept Generalizations
- Systems have parts (elements).
- Systems have boundaries.
- Systems have inputs and outputs.
- The interactions and outputs of a system change when its inputs, elements, or boundaries change.

Key Science Concepts
- Simple machines are tools that make work easier.
- There are six different simple machines.
- Compound machines combine two or more simple machines.
- Motion is an object's direction and speed.
- Changes in speed or direction of motion are caused by forces.
- Friction is a force that opposes motion.
- Moving objects have kinetic energy.
- Objects capable of kinetic energy due to their position have potential energy.

Scientific Investigation Skills and Processes
- Tell others what was found.

Assessment "Look Fors"
- Students can identify and explain the parts of their invention as it relates to systems.
- Students can classify, sort, and label the six different simple machines.
- Students can explain or demonstrate friction, force, motion, direction, kinetic and potential energy, and speed as they relate to simple and compound machines.

Materials/Resources/Equipment
- Copies of Handout 15A (Systems Invention Review), one per student
- One sentence strip with each of the essential science understandings
- Materials from the simple machines center

Implementing the Lesson

Procedures for the presentation portion of the lesson

1. Remind students that they are thinking and acting like scientists. During the presentations, they should behave accordingly. Pass out index cards and encourage students to take notes and/or jot down questions while their peers are presenting. Encourage students to think about how their peers have acted as scientists. They should pay attention to how the inventions are systems. Remind students that they are being evaluated according to the rubric that they were given when the project was assigned.
2. Ask one student to evaluate another student's invention so that all students have a student evaluation and a teacher evaluation.
3. Proceed with the presentations.
4. In their log books, have students respond to the following prompt:
   - Which invention is the most valuable? Why?

Procedures for the review portion of the lesson

1. Ask students to reflect on the invention fair and their products.
2. Tell students that, as you complete the unit on simple machines, you would like to take some time to review what has been learned.
3. Write the following statements on sentence strips, one statement per strip:
   - Simple machines are tools that make work easier.
   - There are six different simple machines.
   - Motion is an object's direction and speed.
   - Compound machines combine two or more simple machines.
   - Friction is a force that opposes motion.
   - Changes in speed or direction of motion are caused by forces.
   - Moving objects have kinetic energy.
   - Objects capable of kinetic energy due to their position have potential energy.

4. Divide the class into eight different groups. Give each group a sentence strip with one of the key science concepts written on it. Explain that the groups will be the teachers for their given concepts. Tell each group that it may go to the simple machine center or use materials readily available in the classroom to demonstrate the concept written on its sentence strip. Explain that students will have no more than 15 minutes to prepare. Each group will then have 2 minutes to demonstrate its concept in some way.
5. Allow groups time to share their statement and how they chose to illustrate or provide an example of the concept. Clarify misconceptions as necessary.
6. Write the following words on the board:
   - Friction, distance, speed, forces, motion, kinetic and potential energy, compound machine, simple machine, lever, pulley, screw, wedge, wheel and axle, inclined plane, and work
   - Ask students how they would use these words to create a concept map. What linking words would they use? As students discuss their responses, put their ideas into a concept map on the board, guiding students' thinking as necessary.

7. Provide each student with a copy of Handout 15A. Tell students to reflect on their invention from the unit. Have them justify how their invention was a system by writing in the parts of the system in the appropriate boxes. Finally,

at the bottom of the page, instruct students to write a sentence about what happens to the system if the inputs, elements, or boundaries change. Provide an example.

8. Allow students to share their system ideas with the class as time allows.

Concluding and Extending the Lesson

Concluding Questions and/or Actions

- In their log books, ask students to respond to the following prompts:
    - My favorite part of this unit was . . .
    - I learned that . . .
    - I still want to know more about . . .
    - Next time I would recommend . . .

What to Do at Home

- Have students visit the website http://www.rubegoldberg.com and examine some of the inventions using simple and compound machines. Encourage students to try to create a Rube Goldberg-type invention at home.

Name:________________________________ Date:____________

Handout 15A

Systems Invention Review

My Invention: ____

Boundaries:

Elements:

Inputs:

Outputs:

Interactions:

If I changed __________________ on my invention, the interactions and output would change by____.

Lesson 16:
Wrap It Up!

Planning the Lesson

Instructional Purpose

- To continue reviewing the unit principles, including key science concepts and concept generalizations.
- To summarize content, scientific process, and conceptual understanding.

Instructional Time

- 45 minutes

Systems Concept Generalizations

- Systems have parts (elements).
- Systems have boundaries.
- Systems have inputs and outputs.
- The interactions and outputs of a system change when its inputs, elements, or boundaries change.

Key Science Concepts

- Simple machines are tools that make work easier.
- There are six different simple machines.
- Compound machines combine two or more simple machines.
- Motion is an object's direction and speed.
- Changes in speed or direction of motion are caused by forces.
- Friction is a force that opposes motion.
- Moving objects have kinetic energy.
- Objects capable of kinetic energy due to their position have potential energy.

Scientific Investigation Skills and Processes

- Make observations.
- Ask questions.
- Learn more.
- Design and conduct the experiment.
- Create meaning.
- Tell others what was found.

Assessment "Look Fors"

- Students can provide examples of systems.
- Students can define motion, force, kinetic and potential energy, and friction and state examples.
- Students can identify and classify various types of simple machines.
- Students can use the scientific investigation processes used by scientists.

Materials/Resources/Equipment

- Student log books
- (optional) Computer

Implementing the Lesson

1. Review student log book prompts from the previous lesson.
2. Wrap up the student log books:
   - Review the log books with the students. Show them a segment from Darwin's or Salk's log to give them the idea that all scientists use logs in their work. Discuss any questions about log entries that they have.

3. Wrap up the content:
   - Ask students to work with a partner to make a concept map of what they have learned in this unit. Give them a topic word to begin or a question to respond to in concept map form.

4. Wrap up the investigation process:
   - Review the steps of the Wheel of Scientific Investigation
   - Work through the steps of the wheel and discuss:
     - What questions have we asked?
     - What data sources have we used in the unit?
     - What types of hypotheses have we made?
     - What were some of our findings?
     - What did we learn from the investigations?

5. Wrap up the systems concept:
   - Ask the students to describe a machine system in their own words and draw one. Then have them share their descriptions with a partner and discuss. Ask three pairs to share in the room.
   - Ask the students: How are the descriptions and drawings similar and different? Can we add components to the machine systems that we have studied?
   - (optional) Create a class machine system to display in the room.

Concluding and Extending the Lesson

Concluding Questions

- In what ways has your thinking changed about force and motion and machines based on our investigations?
- What have you learned about systems?

What to Do at Home

- Have students take their log books and other unit materials home. Tell them to share what they have learned with their family.

Postassessment Directions for the Teacher

Planning the Lesson

Instructional Purpose

- To assess student knowledge of the concept of systems, student understanding of the unit content about simple machines, and student skills in the scientific investigation process.

Instructional Time

- Macroconcept assessment: 20 minutes
- Key science concepts assessment: 30 minutes
- Scientific process assessment: 20 minutes

Materials/Resources/Equipment

- Copies of postassessments for the unit (Postassessment for Systems Concept, Postassessment for Key Science Concepts, and Postassessment for Scientific Process), one per student
- Copies of blank Concept Map: Simple Machines, one per student
- Copies of Exemplar Answers for Systems Concept Postassessment, Exemplar Concept Maps of Simple Machines, and Exemplar Answers for Scientific Process Postassessment for your use
- Pencils
- Large chart paper
- Drawing paper for each student

Implementing the Lesson

1. Give each student a copy of the postassessments to complete in the order noted above. The assessments should take no more than 70 minutes in all.
2. Explain that the assessments will be used to see how much students have learned during the unit.

Scoring

- Use the rubrics contained in the preassessment sections for concept, content, and scientific process. Sample exemplar responses are provided after each postassessment.

Name:______________________________ Date:___________

Postassessment for Systems Concept

1. Give five examples of things that are systems.

____

____

____

____

____

2. Draw one example of a system that you know.

3. Label at least five features of your system.

4. What are three things you can say about *all* systems?

All systems ______________________________

____

All systems ______________________________

____

All systems ______________________________

____

Exemplar Answers for Systems Concept Postassessment

High Score

1. Give five examples of things that are systems.
   Car, aquarium, school, computer, T.V., person
2. Draw one example of a system that you know.
   Computer
3. Label at least five features of your system.
   Boundaries, Input, Output, Batteries, Electric
4. What are three things you can say about *all* systems?
   They have boundaries. They have outputs. They have inputs.

Medium Score

1. Give five examples of things that are systems.
   Us/People, Animal, Car, Flower, Tree
2. Draw one example of a system that you know.
   Tree
3. Label at least five features of your system.
   Leaves, Bark, the Crown, Roots, Branches/or flower sometimes
4. What are three things you can say about *all* systems?
   Can change one way or another, have parts, can break or die

Low Score

1. Give five examples of things that are systems.
   Screw, lever, pulley, wedge
2. Draw one example of a system that you know.
   Unclear—possibly a flower/tree or a skull and spinal cord
3. Label at least five features of your system.
   No labels.
4. What are three things you can say about *all* systems?
   Are different. Are pointy.

Postassessment for Key Science Concepts

Directions to the Teacher: Read the following paragraph to the students.

Today I would like you to think about all the things you know about simple machines. Think about the words you would use and the pictures you could draw to make a concept map. Think about the connections you can make. On your concept map paper, draw in pictures and words what you know about simple machines. You will be drawing a concept map similar to those you have done before.

Name:________________________ Date:____________

Concept Map

Simple Machines

Exemplar Concept Maps of Simple Machines

High Score

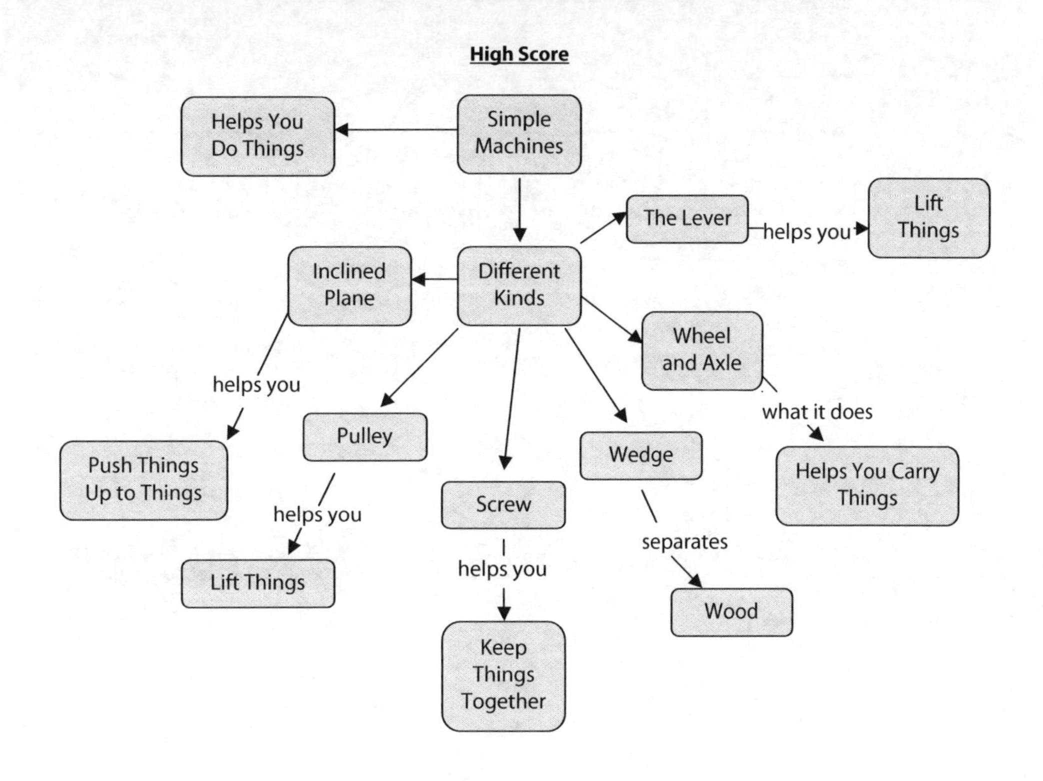

Medium Score

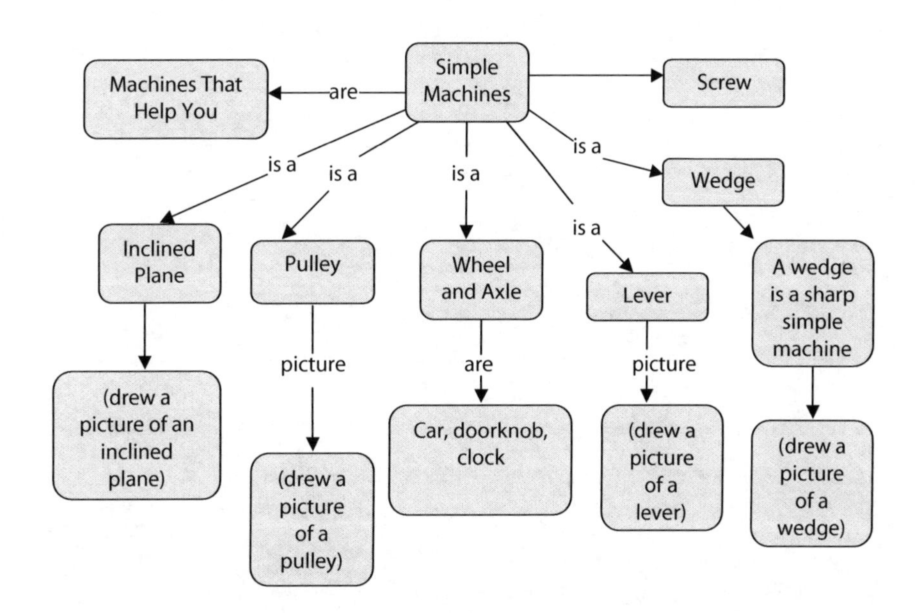

Low Score

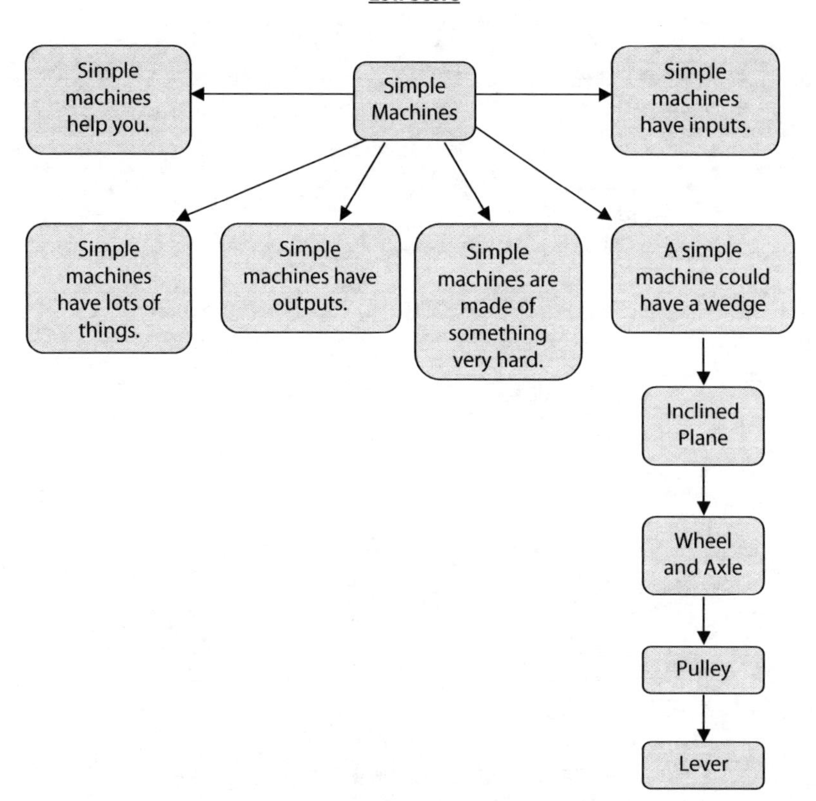

Simple Machines
Simple machines help you.
Simple machines have inputs.
Simple machines have lots of things.
Simple machines have outputs.
Simple machines are made of something very hard.
A simple machine could have a wedge
Inclined Plane
Wheel and Axle
Pulley
Lever

Name:______________________________ Date:___________

Postassessment for Scientific Process

Directions: How would you study the question: How much water do plants need? Describe an experiment to test this question that includes the following:

1. Prediction regarding the question (How much water do plants need?):

   I predict that ____

   ____

   ____

   ____.

2. What materials will be needed to conduct the experiment?

   ____________________ ____________________

   ____________________ ____________________

   ____________________ ____________________

3. What steps must be taken to conduct the experiment and *in what order*?

   a. ____

   b. ____

   c. ____

   d. ____

   e. ____

4. What data do you want to collect and how should it be recorded?

What will I collect?	How will I record the data?

5. How do the data help me decide if my prediction is correct? Explain.

____

____

____

____

Exemplar Answers for Scientific Process Postassessment

High Score

1. Prediction regarding the question (How much water do plants need?):
   I predict that plants need a ½ cup of water for the day.
2. What materials will be needed to conduct the experiment?
   Seeds, water, soil, sun, shovel
3. What steps must be taken to conduct the experiment and *in what order*?
   (a) Dig a hole with the shovel. (b) Put the seeds in the hole. (c) Cover it with soil. (d) Water the plant every day. (e) And make sure it gets a lot of sunlight.
4. What data do you want to collect and how should they be recorded?
   What will I collect? fresh water, sunlight, seeds, soil, shovel
   How will I record the data? (1) Make a hole with the shovel. (2) Put the seeds in the hole. (3) Cover the seeds with the soil. (4) And remember to water it every day. (5) And make sure it gets lots of sunlight. Good luck.
5. How do the data help me decide if my prediction is correct? Explain.
   By trying it out and make sure it grows in a month or 5 weeks.

Medium Score

1. Prediction regarding the question (How much water do plants need?):
   I predict that two cups a day—small.
2. What materials will be needed to conduct the experiment?
   Cups, soil, vase, sun, flower, arch
3. What steps must be taken to conduct the experiment and *in what order*?
   (a) You need a cup, small cup. (b) Get vase and put water in the vase. (c) Get the soil and put in the vase.
4. What data do you want to collect and how should they be recorded?
   What will I collect? Soil and put it in the vase and get water and put in vase and put the flower in it and give it sun.
   How will I record the data? (blank)
5. How do the data help me decide if my prediction is correct? Explain.
   By helping me see it grow.

Low Score

1. Prediction regarding the question (How much water do plants need?).
   I predict that 3 cups a day.
2. What materials will be needed to conduct the experiment?
   Water, shovel, sunlight, soil, seed
3. What steps must be taken to conduct the experiment and *in what order*?
   (a) First you need soil. (b) Then you need a seed. (b) After that you need a shovel. (d) After that you need water. (e) The last thing you need is lots and lots of sunlight.
4. What data do you want to collect and how should they be recorded?
   What will I collect? clocks
   How will I collect the data? by color
5. How do the data help me decide if my prediction is correct? Explain.
   I just thought in my brain and it was correct.

Appendix A
Concept Paper on Systems

By Beverly T. Sher, Ph.D.

This paper was adapted from: Sher, B. T. (2004). Systems. In J. VanTassel-Baska (Ed.), *Science key concepts*. Williamsburg, VA: Center for Gifted Education, The College of William and Mary.

A system is a collection of things and processes that interact with each other and together constitute a meaningful whole. Examples from the realm of science include atoms, chemical reaction systems, individual cells, organs, organ systems, organisms, ecosystems, solar systems, and galaxies; nonscience examples include sewer systems, political systems, the banking system, transportation systems, and so on. All systems share certain properties. These include:

1. Systems have identifiable elements.
2. Systems have definable boundaries.
3. Most systems receive input in the form of material or information from outside their boundaries and generate output to the world outside their boundaries.
4. The interactions of a system's elements with each other and their response to input from outside the system combine to determine the overall nature and behavior of the system.

Figure A1 provides an illustration of how systems work.

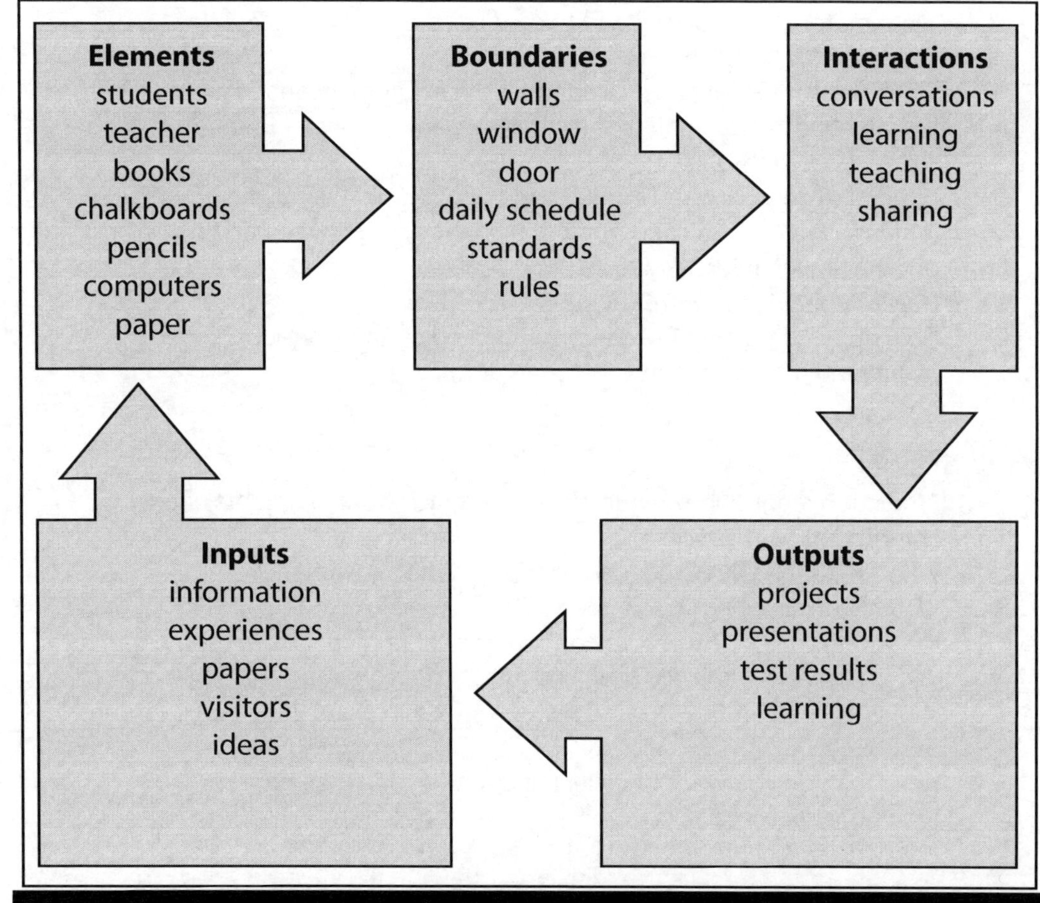

Figure A1. How systems work.

Systems are made up of identifiable elements and processes. The elements comprising an ecosystem, for example, include all of the organisms present as well as all of the physical features of the area that the ecosystem occupies. The elements of a forest ecosystem would include the different trees, bushes, and smaller plants; the insects, birds, and other animals present; the nature of the terrain; the quality of the soil; the availability of water; the weather; and so on. Defining the elements of an ecosystem thoroughly is a large task. Similarly, the elements of nonscience systems are clearly definable. A school system would include all of the physical property appertaining to the schools and their administration: schools, playgrounds, buses, administration buildings, and so on. It also includes all of the teachers, pupils, administrators, and (ideally) parents.

The boundaries of systems also must be defined. The boundaries of an ecosystem are defined physically: they are the boundaries of the territory that it occupies. Thus, the boundary of a forest ecosystem is the edge of the forest. An ecosystem's boundaries can be drawn somewhat arbitrarily; one can speak of a backyard ecosystem or of the planetary ecosystem. The first ecosystem would thus be an element of the second ecosystem. The appropriate choice of boundaries for an ecosystem depends on the phenomena that one wishes to study: To study global warming, it is necessary to include the whole planet, but a study of the effects of man on the alpine tundra could involve only a single mountaintop. Similarly, the boundaries of nonscience systems can be defined in somewhat arbitrary ways, depending on the nature of the process under study. The boundaries of a school system could be chosen to exclude neighboring systems and the federal government. Although all of these elements can affect the school system, they really are not integral to its behavior.

Drawing the boundaries of a system appropriately can reveal much about its nature and behavior. Including phenomena and elements that are irrelevant to the properties under study will make understanding the system unnecessarily difficult. For example, including detailed consideration of the daily actions of members of the Williamsburg City Council in a study of the overall behavior of the American political system adds variables that are probably insignificant for the behavior of the system as a whole and therefore makes the study of the system unnecessarily difficult. Excluding the press from the system, however, probably decreases the understanding of the system, even though the press is not a formally defined branch of government. Although the press could be considered as an external actor that produces input into the system, in practice the actions of the press are so tightly intermeshed with the actions of those that run the government that excluding the press from the government system would make understanding the system more difficult rather than less.

As discussed in *Science for All Americans* (Rutherford & Ahlgren, 1990), one of the best examples of the importance of properly defining the boundaries and elements of an experimental system is Louis Pasteur's elegant experimental solution for the problem of the spontaneous generation of living organisms. Before the 19th century, it was widely believed that living organisms arose spontaneously from nonliving matter, without benefit of the action of other living things. Rats and mice were thought to arise spontaneously from old rags, maggots from old meat. In the 1800s, Louis Pasteur approached this problem experimentally and resolved it. He showed that if flies were kept from contact with meat, no maggots subsequently arose from it; and if meat broth was boiled and then kept in sealed flasks or in flasks that allowed the entry of air but not of dust particles, then the broth did not spoil. By drawing the boundaries of his experimental system to exclude certain elements (namely flies and bacteria), Pasteur proved that meat alone was insufficient to generate maggots and meat broth alone did not spoil. Thus, the doctrine of spontaneous generation was laid to rest.

Another example of the importance of correctly understanding the boundaries and elements integral to a system comes from the controversy over the origin of life on Earth. The science of thermodynamics has been used (inappropriately) to argue that life could not have evolved from nonliving chemicals through simple life forms and up to the many complex forms that we see today; this argument is based on a misunderstanding of the boundaries of the system in which life evolved and an incomplete understanding of thermodynamics. Thermodynamics is the science that sets the limits on energy efficiency and possible outcome of physical and chemical processes. The three laws of thermodynamics can be summarized as follows:

1. Energy can neither be created nor destroyed, only transferred or changed from one form to another.
2. In an irreversible process, the entropy (degree of disorder) of the universe increases; only in a reversible process will it stay constant. The entropy of the universe cannot decrease.
3. At the temperature absolute zero, the entropy of perfect crystals and compounds is zero.

The second law of thermodynamics has been misused to argue that life could not possibly have evolved, because over time the complexity of living things has increased, and hence the system of life on Earth has become more ordered, not more disordered. The basic flaw in this argument is that its proponents have neglected to include the sun in their calculations. Solar energy is the source of most of the energy used by organisms; thus, the thermodynamic properties of the sun must be included in the system. The net entropy of the sun has increased by a degree that is orders of magnitude greater than the degree of entropy decrease caused by the origin and actions of all life on Earth; thus, the entropy of the universe has increased, as it theoretically should.

A third fundamental property of systems is that they can receive input from and act on the world outside their boundaries. Input into a school system, for example, includes federal financial and material assistance. Output from a school system includes educated students. Input into an ecosystem includes things such as solar energy; output from an ecosystem includes things such as carbon dioxide released into the atmosphere as a result of animal respiration and oxygen released by plants.

The final fundamental property of a system is that its overall behavior depends on the properties and interactions of its parts. For example, understanding the behavior of an ecosystem (e.g., whether it is stable or likely to change, whether it is delicate and sensitive to the incursions of man, or whether it can survive human influence with few changes) depends upon understanding the roles of the different elements in the ecosystem and their interactions. Thus, prediction of the number of deer that can be safely hunted in a given area depends upon knowing how fast they reproduce, which wild predators are present and what percentage of the deer population they kill, whether disease is present in the deer population and likely to reduce numbers substantially, which plants the deer use for food and how many deer the plant population can support without being reduced too far to replace itself, and so on.

This dependence of the behavior of the whole system on the properties and interactions of its parts also is seen in nonscience systems. The behavior of the federal government depends on the actions and motivations of its members, their interactions with each other, and their reactions to input from their constituents and from the outside world. The behavior of the local sewer system depends on the amount of material it receives, the age of the pipes, the capacity of the treatment plant, and so on. Attempting to understand the behavior of the whole system based on the nature of its parts is the essence of the philosophy of reductionism, which has been a highly successful approach to the study of systems in general.

Rationale for Teaching the Concept

The understanding of the behavior of one system will help understanding of other systems. Defining the elements, boundaries, inputs, and outputs of a system helps to understand its behavior as a whole. Once a child has learned to do this for a simple system, he or she will be able to apply the process to other, more complex systems. This will help the child understand the scientific process, as setting up successful experiments involves determining which elements should be included and paying close attention to the inputs and outputs of the system; varying the elements present in the experimental system may well change the experimental outcome in ways that illuminate the functioning of the system. More generally, the study of certain scientific systems will deepen a child's understanding of the world around him or her. Every child should have some understanding of the ecosystem of which he or she is an element and the solar system in which he or she resides.

Suggested Applications

There are two different ways to approach the concept of systems with children. The first involves weaving it into the experimental work that they do in the course of their science studies. Defining the experimental system thoroughly and paying attention to the essential variables in the system and excluding the others from consideration are activities critical to any lab science course. The second approach to the concept involves teaching them about some basic scientific systems. Many scientific systems are accessible to children, at least at a simple level. These include systems from many disciplines, including chemistry, geology, biology, and astronomy, as listed (albeit in incomplete fashion) below:

Biology

- ecosystems
- organ systems
- organisms: physiology, behavior

Chemistry

- chemical reaction systems

Geology

- the planet Earth as a geological system: plate tectonics and its manifestations
- geologic change in mountain ranges, river systems, and the like

Meteorology

- weather systems

Astronomy

- solar systems
- galaxies
- Earth-moon system

Problem-Based Learning

The following is an example of a problem-based learning situation that could be used to illustrate the system concept.

The Problem: You own a gardening store. Several townspeople have signed a petition asking you to stop selling some of your products. What should you do?

Areas for students to explore:

1. The garden as a system: look at the interactions of the plants and animals present and seek to minimize animal and disease destruction of the plants.
2. Organic farming techniques
3. Resistant plant varieties
4. Plant varieties that are suitable for the local area's soil conditions, sun-shade conditions, and weather patterns.

Activities for Students: Plant and tend two gardens: an organic garden and a garden in which chemical fertilizers, insecticides, and herbicides are used. Record the amount and kinds of work needed to maintain each; the amounts of chemicals used in the chemical garden; and the yields of the different fruits, vegetables, and flowers planted in each. Report results.

Appendix B
Teaching Models

Introduction to the Teaching Models

Several teaching models are incorporated into the Project Clarion units. These models ensure emphasis on unit outcomes and support student understanding of the concepts and processes that are the focus of each unit. Teachers should become familiar with these models and how to use them before teaching the unit. The models are listed below and outlined in the pages that follow.

1. Frayer Model of Vocabulary Development
2. Taba Model of Concept Development
3. Concept Mapping
4. Wheel of Scientific Investigation and Reasoning

Frayer Model of Vocabulary Development

The Frayer Model (Frayer, Frederick, & Klausmeier, 1969) provides students with a graphic organizer that asks them to think about and describe the meaning of a word or concept. This process enables them to strengthen their understanding of vocabulary words. Through the model, students are required to consider the important characteristics of the word and to provide examples and nonexamples of the concept. This model has similarities to the Taba Model of Concept Development (1962).

In introducing the Frayer Model to your students, demonstrate its use on large chart paper. Begin with a word all students know, such as rock, umbrella, or shoe, placing it on the graphic model. First, ask the students to define the word in their own words. Record a definition that represents their common knowledge. Next, ask students to give specific characteristics of the word/concept or facts they know about it. Record these ideas. Then ask students to offer examples of the idea and then nonexamples to finish the graphic (see Figure B1).

Another way to use the Frayer Model is to provide students with examples and nonexamples and ask them to consider what word or concept is being analyzed. You can provide similar exercises by filling in some portions of the graphic and asking students to complete the remaining sections.

As students share ideas, note the level of understanding of the group and of individual students. As the unit is taught, certain vocabulary words may need this type of expanded thinking to support student readiness for using the vocabulary in the science activities. You may want students to maintain individual notebooks of words so that they can refer back to them in their work.

Taba Model of Concept Development

Each Project Clarion unit supports the development of a specific macroconcept (change or systems). The concept development model, based upon the work of Hilda Taba (1962), supports student learning of the macroconcept. The model involves both inductive and deductive reasoning processes. Used as an early lesson in the unit, the model focuses on the creation of generalizations about the macroconcept from a student-derived list of created concept examples. The model includes a series

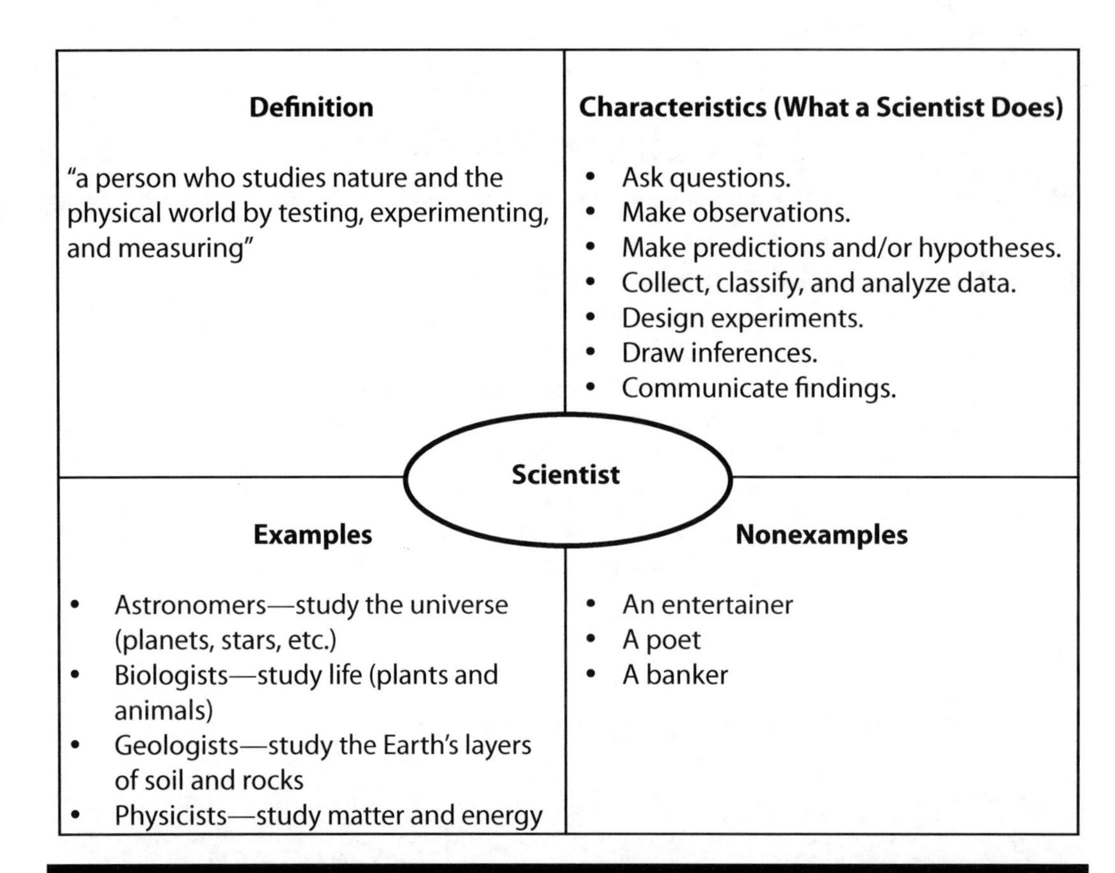

Figure B1. Completed graphic organizer for Frayer Model.

of steps, in which each step involves student participation. Students begin with a broad concept, determine specific examples of the broad concept, create appropriate categorization systems, cite nonexamples of the concept, establish generalizations based on their understanding, and then apply the generalizations to their readings and other situations.

The model generally is most effective when small groups of students work through each step, with whole-class debriefing following each stage of the process. However, with primary-age students, additional teacher guidance may be necessary, especially for the later stages of the model. The steps of the model are outlined below, using the unit concept of change.

1. Students generate examples of the concept of change, derived from their own understanding and experiences with change in the world. Teachers should encourage students to provide at least 15–20 examples; a class list may be created out of the small-group lists to lengthen the set of changes students have to work with.
2. Students then group their changes into categories. This process allows students to search for interrelatedness and to organize their thinking. It often is helpful to have individual examples written on cards so that the categorization may occur physically as well as mentally or in writing. Students should then explain their reasoning for their categorization system and seek clarification from each other as a whole group. Teachers should ensure that all examples have been accounted for in the categorization system established.
3. Students then generate a list of nonexamples of the concept of change. Teachers may begin this step with the direction, "Now list examples of things that *do not change*." Encourage students to think carefully about their

nonexamples and discuss ideas within their groups. Each group should list five to six nonexamples.

4. The students next determine generalizations about the concept of change, using their lists of examples, categories, and nonexamples. Teachers should then share the unit generalizations and relate valid student generalizations to the unit list. Both lists should be posted in the room throughout the course of the unit.
5. During the unit, students are asked to identify specific examples of the generalizations from their own readings, or to describe how the concept applies to a given situation about which they have read. Students also are asked to apply the generalizations to their own writings and their own lives. Several lessons employ a chart that lists several of the generalizations and asks students to supply examples specifically related to the reading or activity of that lesson.

Concept Mapping

A concept map is a graphic representation of one's knowledge on a particular topic. Concept maps support learning, teaching, and evaluation (Novak & Gowin, 1984). Students clarify and extend their own thinking about a topic. Teachers find concept mapping useful for envisioning the scope of a lesson or unit. They also use student-developed concept maps as a way of measuring their progress. Meaningful concept maps often begin with a particular question (focus question) about a topic, event, or object.

Concept maps were developed in 1972 by Dr. Joseph Novak at Cornell University as part of his research about young children's understanding of science concepts. Students were interviewed by researchers who recorded their responses. The researchers sought an effective way to identify changes in students' understanding over time. Novak and his research colleagues began to represent the students' conceptual understanding in concept maps because learning takes place through the assimilation of new concepts and propositions into existing conceptual and propositional frameworks.

Concept maps show concepts and relationships between them. (See the sample concept map in Figure B2.) The concepts are contained within boxes or oval shapes and the connections between concepts are represented by lines with linking words.

Concepts are the students' perceived ideas generalized from particular experiences. Sometimes the concepts placed on the map may contain more than one word. Words placed on the line link words or phrases. The propositions contain two or more concepts connected by linking words or phrases to form a meaningful statement.

The youngest students may view and develop concept maps making basic connections. They may begin with two concepts joined by a linking word. These "sentences" (propositions) become the building blocks for concept maps. Older students may begin to make multiple connections immediately as they develop their maps.

As students map their knowledge base, they begin to represent their conceptual understanding in a hierarchical manner. The broadest, most inclusive concepts often are found at the top of a concept map. More specific concepts and examples then follow.

Each Project Clarion unit contains an overview concept map, showing the essential knowledge included in the lessons and the connections students should be able to make as a result of their experiences within the unit. This overview may be useful as a classroom poster that the teacher and students may refer to throughout the unit.

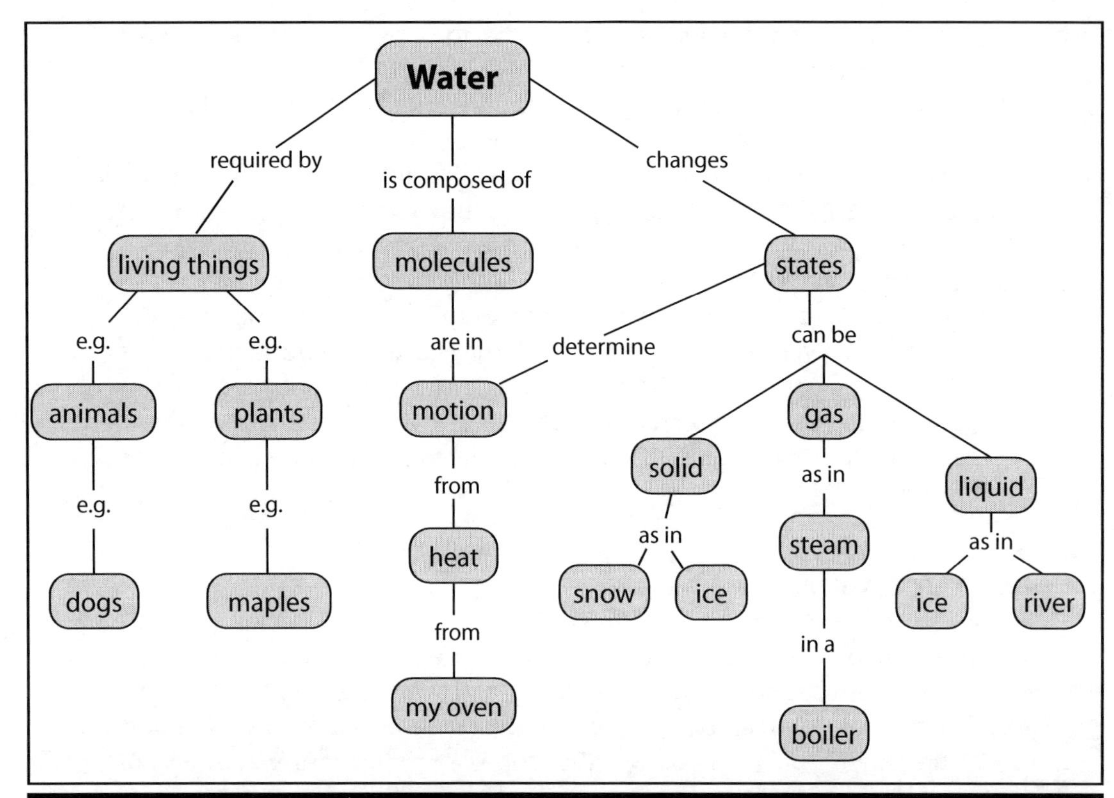

Figure B2. A concept map showing a student's understanding of water.

Note. Adapted from Novak and Gowin (1984).

Strategies to Prepare Students for Concept Mapping

The following strategies can be incorporated to help prepare your students for concept mapping activities (Novak & Gowin, 1984).

What Do Words Mean?

1. Ask students to picture in their minds some common words (e.g., water, tree, door, box, pencil, dog). Start with "object" words, saying them one at a time, allowing time for students to picture each of them.
2. Create a class list of object words, asking students to name other objects they can picture in their minds to add to the list.
3. Next create a list of event words (e.g., jumping, running, eating). Ask students to envision each of these in their minds and encourage them to contribute to the class list of event words.
4. Give students a few words that are likely to be unfamiliar to most of them, asking if they can see a picture in their mind. These words should be short (e.g., data, cell, prey, inertia). You might include a few simple words in another language. Ask students if they have any mind pictures.
5. Discuss the fact that words are useful to us because they convey meaning. This only happens when people can form a picture in their mind that represents the meaning they connect with the word.

What Is a Concept?

1. Introduce the word *concept* and explain that concept is the word we use to mean some kind of object or event we can picture in our mind. Refer back to the word lists previously developed as you discuss the word and ask if these

are concepts. Can students see a picture in their mind for each of them? Let students know that when they come upon a word they do not know well enough to form a picture, they will just need to learn the concept associated with that new word.

2. Provide each table with picture cards and ask students to take turns at their table naming some of the concepts included in the card.

What Are Linking Words?

1. Prepare a list of words such as *the, is, are, when, that, then.* Ask students if they can see a picture in their mind for each of these words. Explain that these are not concept words. These are linking words we use when we speak or write to link concept words together into sentences that have special meaning. Ask students if they have any words to add to the list. Label the list "Linking Words."
2. Hold up two picture cards (sky and blue) and give students a sample sentence ("The sky is blue.") Ask students to tell you the concept words and the linking words in your sentence. Give another example.
3. Give each pair of students a few picture cards. Ask the students to work with partners to pick up two cards and then develop a sentence that links the two cards. They should take turns, with one partner making the sentence and the other identifying the concepts and the linking words. Ask them to repeat this a few times and then have several partners share their sentences.
4. Explain to students that it is easy to make up sentences and to read sentences where the printed labels (words) are familiar to them. Explain that reading and writing sentences is like making a link between two things (concepts) they already know. Practice this idea during reading time, asking students to find a sentence and analyze it for concepts and linking words.

Wheel of Scientific Investigation and Reasoning

All scientists work to improve our knowledge and understanding of the world. In the process of scientific inquiry, scientists connect evidence with logical reasoning. Scientists also apply their imaginations as they devise hypotheses and explanations that make sense of the evidence. Students can strengthen their understanding of particular science topics through investigations that cause them to employ evidence gathering, logical reasoning, and creativity. The Wheel of Scientific Investigation and Reasoning contains the specific processes involved in scientific inquiry to guide students' thinking and actions.

Make Observations

Scientists make careful observations and try things out. They must describe things as accurately as possible so that they can compare their observations from one time to another and so that they can compare their observations with those of other scientists. Scientists use their observations to form questions for investigation.

Ask Questions

Scientific investigations usually are initiated through a problem to be solved or a question asked. Selecting just the right question or clearly defining the problem to be addressed is critical to the investigation process.

Learn More

To clarify their questions, scientists learn more by reviewing bodies of scientific knowledge documented in text and previously conducted investigations. Also, when scientists get conflicting information they make fresh observations and insights that may result in revision of the previously formed question. By learning more, scientists can design and conduct more effective experiments or build upon previously conducted experiments.

Design and Conduct the Experiment

Scientists use their collection of relevant evidence, their reasoning, and their imagination to develop a hypothesis. Sometimes scientists have more than one possible explanation for the same set of observations and evidence. Often when additional observations and testing are completed, scientists modify current scientific knowledge.

To test out hypotheses, scientists design experiments that will enable them to control conditions so that their results will be reliable. Scientists repeat their experiments, doing it the same way it was done before and expecting to get very similar, although not exact, results. It is important to control conditions in order to make comparisons. Scientists sometimes are not sure what will happen because they don't know everything that might be having an effect on the experiment's outcome.

Create Meaning

Scientists analyze the data that are collected from the experiment to add to the existing body of scientific knowledge. They organize their data using data tables and graphs and then make inferences from the data to draw conclusions about whether their question was answered and the effectiveness of their experiments. Scientists also create meaning by comparing what they found to existing knowledge. The analysis of data often leads to identification of related questions and future experiments.

Tell Others What Was Found

In the investigation process, scientists often work as a team, sharing findings with each other so that they may benefit from the results. Initially, individual team members complete their own work and draw their own conclusions.

One way to introduce the wheel to students is to provide them with the graphic model (see Figure B3) and ask them to tell one reason why each section of the wheel is important to scientific investigation.

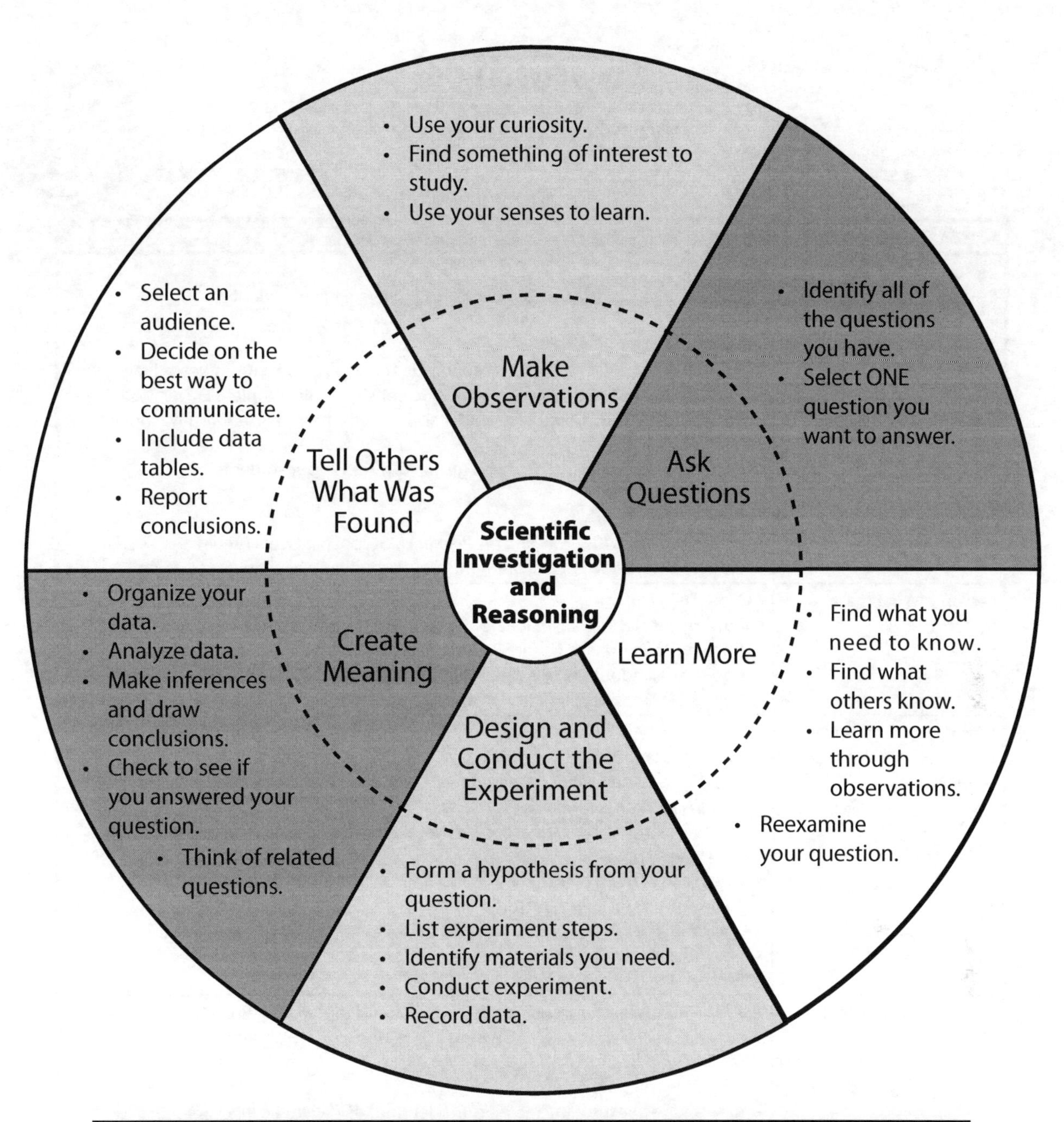

Figure B3. Wheel of Scientific Investigation and Reasoning model.

Note. Adapted from Kramer (1987).

Appendix C
Materials List

Lesson	Materials Needed
Lesson 1: What Is a Scientist?	• Lab coat for teacher • One lab coat (white adult T-shirt or dress shirt) for each student • Beaker • Microscope or magnifying glass • PowerPoint slides, charts, or transparencies of Handouts 1A (Completed Frayer Model of Vocabulary Development on Scientists), 1B (Incomplete Frayer Model of Vocabulary Development on Scientists), and 1C (Wheel of Scientific Investigation and Reasoning) • One chart of Handout 1B for each group of three or four students • Markers • Student log books • *Professor Aesop's the Crow and the Pitcher* by Stephanie Gwyn Brown • Word wall cards: scientist, communicate, observation, question, experiment
Lesson 2: What Is a System?	• Model of a car • PowerPoint slides, transparencies, or charts of Handouts 2A (Picture of a Car), 2B (System Definitions), 2C (Car Systems Model), and 2D (Understanding Systems) • Copies of Handout 2A, one per group of three or four students • Copies of Handout 2E (Blank Systems Model), one per student
Lesson 3: What Scientists Do—Observe, Question, Learn More	• One toy car and one toy truck per group of three or four students • Charts of Handouts 3A (Completed Wheel of Scientific Investigation and Reasoning) and 3B (Force and Motion Definitions) • Copies Handout 3A (one per student) • Sentence strip with the question, "How does surface type affect speed?" • Chart paper • One piece of foam board • Towel, canvas, or other "textured" material • Masking tape • One ruler • Student log books
Lesson 4: What Scientists Do—Experiment, Create Meaning, Tell Others	• PowerPoint slides, transparencies, or charts of Handouts 4A (Road Surfaces), 4B (Definition of Hypothesis), 4C (Using a Question to Form a Hypothesis), 4D (Steps for Friction Experiment), and 4E (Friction Experiment Data Sheet) • Student copies of Handout 4E • One badge per student created from Handout 4F (Scientific Investigation Badges) • Sentence strip with the question, "How does surface type affect speed?" • Two of the same cars per group of three to four students • Stations that have: four to five foam-board ramps half smooth and half covered in a textured material (e.g., sandpaper, towel, bubble wrap, carpet). Each station should be set up so that students compare a car's motion down a smooth surface versus a coarse surface. • 2 inch, 4 inch, and 6 inch blocks of wood per station • Yardstick or measuring tape per station • One ruler per group of three or four students • Student log books
Lesson 5: Creative Problem Solving	• Chart paper and markers for each group of students • Copies of Handouts 5A (Problem Scenario), 5B (Exploring the Problem), and 5C (Plan of Action), one per group
Lesson 6: The Process of Invention	• Materials for drawing, such as paper, pencils, crayons, markers, or colored pencils

Lesson	Materials Needed
Lesson 7: The Mother of Invention	• PowerPoint slide, transparency, or chart of Handout 7A (My Invention Plans) • Copies of Handouts 7A, 7B (Brainstorming Form), and 7C (Rubric for Invention Creation), one per student • T-Chart created on chart paper with headings "Discovery" and "Invention" • Sentence strip with "'Necessity is the mother of invention'—Plato" • Sentence strips with definitions of discover and invention • Student log books • *Mistakes That Worked* by Charlotte F. Jones
Lesson 8: Introduction to Simple Machines	• PowerPoint slide or transparency of Handout 3A • One copy per student of Handout 8A (Simple Machine Scavenger Hunt) • Copies of a different Rube Goldberg invention drawing for each group • Several types of screws of various sizes, shapes, and number of threads • Several examples of inclined planes varying in height and length • Several examples of pulleys such as fixed, moveable, and block and tackle • Several examples of wedges such as shims, a picture of an ax, scissors, and a zipper • Several examples of levers with the fulcrum in various places such as scissors, binder clips, a shovel, and a stapler
Lesson 9: The Screw and The Wedge	• PowerPoint slide or transparency of Handout 3A • Copies of Handouts 9A (Screw and Wedge Experiment Steps and Hypothesis) and 9B (Screw and Wedge Experiment Data and Conclusion), one per student • Copies of Handouts 9C (Center Extension for Simple Machines Investigation: Screw and Wedge, Activity 1) and 9D (Center Extension for Simple Machines Investigation: Screw and Wedge, Activity 2) for the simple machines center • Several types of screws of various sizes, shapes, and number of threads • Several types of nails with different points • A wooden wedge for each group of three or four students • Two boards of the same size nailed together for each group of three or four students, plus one extra set (nails should be the same length and width) • Two boards of the same size screwed together for each group of three or four students, plus one extra set (screws should be the same length and width) • Examples of wedges: shims, picture of a sledge hammer, scissors that are slanted like a wedge, a zipper • (optional) Lego® Bricks, K'nex, Tinkertoys, different-sized cars and wheels for simple machines center
Lesson 10: The Inclined Plane and the Wheel and Axle	• Handout 8A from previous lesson (student copy, rows 1 and 2 already completed) • PowerPoint slide or transparency of Handout 10A (Examples of Inclined Planes) • Copies of Handout 10B (Making an Inclined Plane for Distance Data Sheet), one per student • One copy each of Handouts 10C (Center Extension for Simple Machines Investigation: Inclined Plane and Wheel and Axle, Activity 1), 10D (Center Extension for Simple Machines Investigation: Inclined Plane and Wheel and Axle, Activity 2), 10E (Center Extension for Simple Machines Investigation: Inclined Plane and Wheel and Axle, Activity 3), and 10F (Center Extension for Simple Machines Investigation: Inclined Plane and Wheel and Axle, Activity 4) for the simple machines center • Piece of blank paper • Scissors • Pencil • Eight dowel rods per group of three or four students • Ruler, tape measure, or yardstick for each group • Sturdy piece of 12" x 24" cardboard for each group (alternatively, you could use double- or triple-reinforced file folders) • One toy car per group of 3-4 students • Masking tape • Different-sized wheels, rods, cardboard, ramps, a doorknob for the students to take apart, and other similar materials for the simple machines center • Rubber bands or a spring weight measure

Lesson	Materials Needed
Lesson 11: The Lever	• Handout 8A, partially completed • PowerPoint slide or transparency of Handouts 3A and 11A (Examples of Levers) • Copies of Handouts 11B (Lever Investigation) and 11C (Lever Data Table), one per student • Lesson 7 handouts for invention planning (Handouts 7A, 7B, 7C, and 7D) • Two rulers for each pair of students • Pen with a cap for each pair of students (or a flat-sided pencil) • Two rolls of pennies for each pair of students (one opened, one closed) • Masking tape
Lesson 12: The Pulley	• Different types of pulleys purchased from a hardware store, including single and block-and-tackle pulleys • 2" x 36" PVC pipe or dowel rods for each group of three or four students • One gallon-size paint can or a gallon water jug filled with liquid for each group of three or four students (must have a handle to tie a rope around) • 15 feet of ¾" or larger rope for each group of three or four students • Copy of Handout 12A (Center Extension for Simple Machines Investigation: Pulleys) for the simple machines center
Lesson 13: Compound Machines	• Handout 8A, completed • PowerPoint slide or transparency of Handout 13A (Examples of Compound Machines) • Handout 13B (Scenarios for Building Machines), with each scenario cut out for the students • Copies of Handouts 13C (Center Extension for Simple Machines Investigation: Complex Machines, Activity 1) and 13D (Center Extension for Simple Machines Investigation: Complex Machines, Activity 2) for the simple machines center • Materials from the simple machines center • Additional building or drawing materials, including pipe cleaners, blank paper, markers, scissors, rope or string, wood sticks or blocks of wood, cardboard of various lengths, and other similar materials
Lesson 14: Final Touches	• PowerPoint slide, transparency, or chart of the Wheel of Scientific Investigation and Reasoning (Handout 3A) • Copies of Handout 14A (My Invention Presentation Form), one per student • Student log books
Lesson 15: Invention Presentations and Conclusion	• Copies of Handout 15A (Systems Invention Review), one per student • One sentence strip with each of the essential science understandings • Materials from the simple machines center
Lesson 16: Wrap It Up!	• Student log books • (optional) Computer

References

Center for Science, Mathematics, and Engineering Education. (1996). *National science education standards.* Washington, DC: National Academy Press.

Fowler, M. (1990). The diet cola test. *Science Scope, 13,* 32–34.

Frayer, D. A., Frederick, W. C., & Klausmeier, H. J. (1969). *A schema for testing the level of concept mastery.* Working Paper from the Wisconsin Research and Development Center for Cognitive Learning, The University of Wisconsin.

Jones, C. F. (1994). *Mistakes that worked.* New York: Doubleday.

Kramer, S. P. (1987). *How to think like a scientist: Answering questions by the scientific method.* New York: T. Y. Crowell.

Novak, J., & Gowin, B. D. (1984). *Learning how to learn.* New York: Cambridge University Press.

Rutherford, F. J., & Ahlgren, A. (1991). *Science for all Americans.* New York: Oxford University Press.

Scholastic. (1996). *Scholastic children's dictionary* (Rev. ed.). New York: Author.

Taba, H. (1962). *Curriculum development: Theory and practice.* New York: Harcourt, Brace.

VanTassel-Baska, J. (1986). Effective curriculum and instructional models for talented students. *Gifted Child Quarterly, 30,* 164–169.

VanTassel-Baska, J., & Little, C. (Eds.). (2003). *Content-based curriculum for gifted learners.* Waco, TX: Prufrock Press.